SOMETHING SPEAKS TO ME

SOMETHING SPEAKS TO ME

Where Criticism Begins

◉

Michel Chaouli

THE UNIVERSITY OF CHICAGO PRESS

Chicago and London

The University of Chicago Press, Chicago 60637
The University of Chicago Press, Ltd., London
© 2024 by The University of Chicago
Published 2024
Printed in the United States of America

33 32 31 30 29 28 27 26 25 24   1 2 3 4 5

ISBN-13: 978-0-226-83031-5 (cloth)
ISBN-13: 978-0-226-83042-1 (paper)
ISBN-13: 978-0-226-83043-8 (e-book)
DOI: https://doi.org/10.7208/chicago/9780226830438.001.0001

Library of Congress Cataloging-in-Publication Data

Names: Chaouli, Michel, 1959– author.
Title: Something speaks to me : where criticism begins / Michel Chaouli.
Other titles: Where criticism begins
Description: Chicago ; London: The University of Chicago Press, 2024. |
    Includes bibliographical references and index.
Identifiers: LCCN 2023025322 | ISBN 9780226830315 (cloth) |
    ISBN 9780226830421 (paperback) | ISBN 9780226830438 (ebook)
Subjects: LCSH: Criticism.
Classification: LCC PN81 .C57 2024 | DDC 801/.95—dc23/eng/20230706
LC record available at https://lccn.loc.gov/2023025322

♾ This paper meets the requirements of ANSI/NISO Z39.48-1992
(Permanence of Paper).

For Jonathan Elmer and Andrew Miller

Contents

To Start

I want to tell you about a mishap I had while teaching Franz Kafka's novel *The Trial* a few years ago. The basics are quickly summarized: after reading out loud a passage that I had chosen because it seemed especially rich, I found I had nothing to say about it. *Nothing*. I tried finessing things by reading it a second time: still nothing. Panic rising, I skipped to another passage I had marked and read it to the class, and then another—always with the same outcome.

This was unnerving. I had set off on one path—the path of analysis and interpretation, the path I knew, or thought I knew—only to find myself repeatedly led back to my starting point, to Kafka's words themselves. It was a bit like walking into a Luis Buñuel movie, *The Exterminating Angel*, for example, or *The Discreet Charm of the Bourgeoisie*, where every attempt at achieving a simple task—crossing a threshold or sitting down to a meal—is mysteriously foiled.

Or like wandering into a story by Kafka himself, a story like "An Imperial Message." It's a simple story: a messenger rushes to get a message from the dying emperor to you—yes, *you*—yet despite his swiftness, despite his resolve, he never manages to leave the palace, much less cross the vast expanse of the empire to reach you. Like *The Trial* and so much of Kafka's writing, the story is pervaded by the feeling that a character's efforts to move forward, vigorous though they may be, result in nothing but futility and exhaustion. It's a feeling we know from bad dreams and one I came to know in front of my class. Try as I might, I found no way to deliver the message.

I have often returned to that moment, and not without dread, since the burn of humiliation never quite heals. One reason to revisit it may be that I soon felt, or perhaps hoped, that the scene betrayed something more than my own shortcoming, that being tongue-tied spoke to a shared condition, the condition of criticism, which we encounter in reviews and monographs but whose roots reach deeper and wider. I felt and hoped that my failure to speak was mute testimony to a general difficulty in saying something that could stand up to the experience of reading the passages from *The Trial*—the difficulty of criticism. This book is a wager that there is something to that feeling and that hope.

Most things I encounter in the world do not impel me to speak about them. When I hold a spoon without saying something about it, I do not feel an absence, a void aching to be filled, a stutter pounding against an invisible barrier, and not because there is nothing to say about it. An inquiry into the spoon need not be less demanding than examining a work by Kafka. When I take the spoon for granted and credit it with indifferent silence, as I do every day, I do lose something: I deprive myself of the knowledge of its place in history and miss out on the pleasure of noticing just how elegant a device this piece of flatware is. But that is not essential to the relationship we have, the spoon and I. Telling its story, singing its praises, or enumerating its flaws, is something I do for my own sake or for the sake of others, not something the spoon asks of me. If it can be said to ask anything of me, it is to use it—to stir the broth or tap the soft-boiled egg; so, I use it. As a rule, the spoon does not call on me to grapple with its significance, which is why as a rule I do not feel the urge to put it down and tell you about it.

Yet when holding a book that speaks to me, that is just what I feel: the urge to put it down and tell you. And when I then fail, my silence feels different from the one with which I greet the spoon. Now my silence consists not in the mere absence of words but has a volume and mass all its own. I feel the pressure of words I am *not* uttering. These are not words I know and have chosen to hold back, the way I decide to keep a secret. They are words whose surging force I feel yet whose shape and character elude me. Because I require them to give shape to my experience, their remaining out of reach means that my own experience fails me: What just happened to me? Did anything happen? Nor must I remain silent to hear the absence of words: often (in the classroom, for instance, or the scholarly study) it is the very abundance of discourse, its polish and erudition, that bears witness to what remains unspoken.

It comes down to this:

> Something speaks to me.
> I must tell you about it.
> But I don't know how.

That is the heart of it—the heart of criticism and its difficulty, no matter its form, no matter its refinement: I read something, and next there is an upsurge of desire to tell you about it. "Desire" is not quite right, since what makes itself felt is something closer to a need, a need so obscure that it remains nameless. It is the need to share what overwhelms me, a feeling that seizes Virginia Woolf when one day, walking in Sussex, she comes across some children playing a game. Here is her diary:

> I caught them at it, as I stood in the road beneath, pink & blue & red & yellow frocks raised above me, & nothing behind them but the vast Asheham hills—a sight too beautiful for one pair of eyes. Instinctively I want someone to catch my overflow of pleasure.[1]

I watch, I hear, I read something, and suddenly there is an overflow of beauty or of some feeling or thought that is too much for my eyes and ears, and I need you to know. But I don't know what exactly to say or how, which is all the more reason I must tell you. Reading (watching, hearing, . . .), I feel called. I also feel called upon: called upon to tell you, because only in telling you do I have a chance to learn how.

We prize the care of scholarly exegesis (and rightly), yet scholarship and exegesis lead but a zombie existence when they fail to be animated by this simple, headstrong urgency to share what is still too unformed to be called an experience. Stanley Cavell, philosopher-poet, describes it in a way that has given shape to my own ways of description:

> I want to tell you something I've seen, or heard, or realized, or come to understand, for the reasons for which such things are communicated. . . . I want to tell you because the knowledge, unshared, is a burden.[2]

It is a familiar feeling—everyone knows it—yet it is also strange. Do I know why or when the urge to speak arises? Why do certain things rouse it but not others (some books or pictures, say, but very few spoons)? Why did it well up yesterday but not today, and why to you but not to me? And suppose I give in to the urge: what do I say? How does my speech and my behavior remain equal to what I have read or seen or heard? When I tell you, does it have to be *you* I tell, or could it be anyone, or no one? (Was Woolf's diary able to catch her overflow of pleasure, or did she need a human being by her side?) Strange how often I feel that I have failed the urge to tell and that you have failed to hear.

And you—do I know you? Sometimes you take on a known shape: a friend, a lover, students in a class, colleagues at a meeting. Sometimes (now, for example) you remain anonymous, an abstract "reader" whom I conjure to get through writing a sentence. At other times you are no person at all. Yet even then, even when I insist that I am just "scribbling notes to myself" or writing for (or to) no one at all, I take part in a world beyond myself. Since language can never be my private domain, I am in the mesh of the public world the moment I seek words that are a match for an encounter with something that holds significance for me. It's like writing an email with the intention of not sending it: every note to myself has the infrastructure of communication built into it. Even when I am not thinking of you, even when I put down the book to write in my diary, I am moved by the need of telling you, which is also the need to go outside myself.

This need, dim and pressing, begins to reveal its design when things get jammed, as they did that day when facing Kafka's *Trial*. When I fail in telling you, when you fail to feel and know what I feel and know, then a bond between us remains unachieved and a rift opens. It is the burden Cavell speaks of. That is one injury. But there is another, perhaps more significant breach, a breach not between us but between what I have read (or watched or heard . . .) and my thoughts and feelings. Not telling you—or, worse, not finding a way to tell you—leaves me with a damaged experience: what I felt and thought while reading (watching, hearing, . . .) comes apart before it has had a chance to gather shape. I am not left alone with my experience as much as I am left without a coherent experience.

Now I see what should have been obvious from the start, namely, that the experience is not available to me like a possession, an entity of known shape and weight ready to be passed on; it is not mine to give you. In most cases, it has not yet earned the title of experience. It is something like a hunch or a potentially interesting disturbance, and only in my telling, and in your hearing, can it take the shape of "experience." Only once I have managed to share it with you, once I have ceded it to a domain beyond myself, do I come to think that it was mine all along. The need to tell you is really the need to discover what I think of as my own experience.

Even when it dazzles with historical or philological insights, criticism worth bothering with remains alive to that obscure moment when I am seized by the urgency to share with you an experience whose outline I no more than dimly sense.

One thing to hold on to, then: Criticism—criticism worth writing and reading, criticism worth saying and hearing—does not provide a transcript of an encounter with a work (of art, of reflection, of any sort or genre) that lies in the past. It is not the eulogy for an experience that has been put to rest. Rather, this criticism is poetic. "The aims and approach of poetic criticism," Friedrich Schlegel writes, are to "replenish the work, rejuvenate it, shape it afresh."[3] (The year is 1798, and this is the first time someone joins the word *poetisch* to *Kritik*, as far as I know.) Parasitic though it may be, belated though it may be, poetic criticism replenishes, rejuvenates, shapes. It *makes* something; it produces, which is just what "poetic" means at root.

And what does poetic criticism make? It makes sense. It is the staging ground on which the encounter with a significant thing—a poetic work—gains form and depth and texture and becomes an experience. It makes (rather than merely documents) my surprise, my insights, my dread, and my delight, my comprehension as well as my incomprehension.

As I set out to make sense of the work I face, I must also make sense of my own capacities, which means that in the best case I bring to light—or just bring about—capacities in myself that allow me to grapple with what the work asks of me. But this is no project of self-improvement, since there is no orderly procedure. If pressed to explain myself, I may go on and on about theories and methods; be sure that such talk goes in one ear and out the other. The fact is that I don't know how to go about criticism, which is not a bug but a feature.

The urgency to tell you, the urgency to make sense of my own thoughts and feelings by going outside myself, the urgency to make myself as I make sense of a thing, this urgency need not slacken once I have found a way to speak. Sometimes—and those are moments of happiness—it transmits itself just as mysteriously as it appeared: when

I set down the book to tell you about it, it can happen (depending on how or what I say, or on your mood, or on what may be on your mind just then, or on an incalculable mix of these variables and others)—it can happen that you, in turn, find yourself roused to speak, to put down *this* book and tell someone about it and make something of your own—not right away, perhaps, and not in a way that stands in clear relation to my speech, but still inspired or incited by it. Defying the laws of matter, the poetic can *gain* in strength as it leaps from body to body.

In fact, this contagious creativity may be the crux of it: we keep searching for the poetic, submitting to painstaking analysis the words on the page, when its power lies not in what the words say but in what they allow to be said—not in the speech produced but in speech unleashed in others. (I speak of words and speech because I know those best, but the work can take any material form: brushstrokes, light, gestures . . .)

Where is this poetic criticism to be found? Wherever there is criticism, which is wherever human beings come across beauty that is too much for one pair of eyes, wherever they find themselves bowled over by joy, by pain, by dread—by forms of significance that overflow systems of meaning—that makes them scramble for words. We tend to give the name criticism to what is produced by scholarship and journalism. Most of what appears under those titles, terrified of being bowled over, braces itself with all the equipment the professional disciplines can afford. But even there you can find poetic criticism. Even starchy scholarship or, more typical in our moment, a discourse choking on righteousness holds somewhere within it a vulnerability to being jolted by a surfeit of sense and feeling. The issue is not that poetic criticism stands against nonpoetic criticism but that, by and large, too little criticism is done poetically. The aim of this book is to bring about more.

Something speaks to me.
I must tell you about it.
But I don't know how.

That's all there is to it: I hear something that urges me to speak, yet when I open my mouth, I do not know what exactly to say or how. Sometimes a way opens, and sometimes my tongue remains tied, and—here lies the strangeness and the power of the phenomenon—it is not always clear which of these is the better way.

I'll call the three steps intimacy, urgency, and opacity.

If something is to speak to me, there must be intimacy between us. That sounds obvious, but it isn't. *The Trial* was written long before I was born, by someone oblivious to my future existence, and yet I must hear it as addressing *me* without falling prey to a delusion. (That would be a false intimacy, which happens all the time.) Something speaks to me not when I know how to decipher signs according to an agreed-upon code but when this something holds significance for me. I may not be able to pin down a meaning (most often I won't), but I must feel that meanings are in play—that what I read *matters*, which just means: matters *to me*. For that to happen, I must be vulnerable to significance. Intimacy is the vulnerability to significance.

Only when there is intimacy between me and some work—a passage, a line, a gesture, a tune—can I feel urged to do something about it. Urgency is the quickening I feel when a work seduces me—or compels me—into changing my place in the world, hence changing myself, if only by a bit. I encounter a thing that speaks to me, and it incites me to act. Urgency is the wellspring of poetic criticism. The aim of criticism is not understanding but action, yet because my action is always caught up with sense, ways of doing (or making) are always entangled in ways of understanding.

How and why something speaks to me and how and why I turn to speak about it or act on it is not something of which I can give a full and faithful account. The encounters, and the significance they hold, remain opaque to me, which is another way of saying that I remain opaque to myself, because something about the thing surpasses my resources. It may not have surpassed me a year earlier when I stood before a group of students, holding the same book open to the same page. Yet here and now, my ways of speaking and of acting are unseated by it: it is too beautiful for words, or too eerie, too simple, too enigmatic, too intense—too something. Being thrown by the thing unnerves me, and sometimes—these are moments of magic and bliss—that sets free new ways of speaking and acting.

It goes without saying (but let's say it anyway) that the three-step of poetic criticism is less like an algorithm and more like a dance, where discrete steps—first one, then two, then three—melt into one fluid motion as I get the hang of it: one-and-two-and-three. Someone learning to play the piano taps out what he or she sees on the sheet, which yields a pileup of notes, not a melody. In a melody, notes do not arrive in isolated succession but herald what is to come as they echo what came before. In poetic criticism, too, each step is utterly active in the other two. If you like, think of them as moments of one arc or dimensions of one act, though these metaphors, too, have their problems.

One of the risks in breaking down a motion into parts is believing that each segment has an independent existence and substance; before you know it the analytic fiction has congealed into a reality of its own. In the pages ahead, I will fall prey to this risk as I dwell on each step. But the idea is not to "explain" or "defend" their validity as autonomous entities that, concatenated, yield a "method." The idea is to learn to walk, maybe to venture a few dance moves.

The three-step looks simple but is difficult to perform. Most of us do what we can to avoid it. Look at what happens in the classroom and in print: here, the chief business of criticism seems to be to keep at bay the force of works whose ability to snap us out of our torpor drew us to them in the first place. How strange it is that we use our skills to erect thick walls—of formal analysis, of historicism, of political and moral wariness—lest we be touched by what, in truth, lures us. Or maybe not so strange, since what lures us is often what is too much for us.

The remedy lies not in becoming unskilled. It lies in forging new skills—unlearning some old skills and honing new ones. It lies in teaching ourselves new ways of speaking about a work that has spoken to us. Perhaps then the difficulty of criticism will not frighten us so.

PART 1

Something Speaks to Me

(INTIMACY)

Every act of real criticism, fancy or artless, polished or rough, takes shape in three basic steps, I said:

Something speaks to me.
I must tell you about it.
But I don't know how.

If one of the steps goes missing—if I fail to hear something speaking to me; if I feel no urge to say or to do something about it; if in the process I do not lose my bearings—criticism is a shell game and not worth the bother. But with all three . . .

Something speaks to me. Step 1 seems straightforward enough, until one notices how hard it can be to notice the phenomenon. Case in point: on the day I stood before my students holding a copy of Kafka's *Trial* (a novel I had taught many times, mind you) and found I had nothing to say about it, I first obsessed about what I am now labeling step 3—being thwarted in speaking—which makes sense. Once the fluster had settled, my worries broadened to include step 2—the felt urge to say something about the text, an urge to which I had proven notably inadequate. But step 1 remained shrouded in obscurity.

With the pebble monopolizing my attention, I found it easy to over-look how well the shoe fit. I failed to recognize that my failure had begun with a success—that the failure was a failure *thanks* to a success: something had spoken to me, and I had heard it speak. Without that initial spark, I would have been spared the misfirings that followed, the failure that preoccupied me long enough to lead to these lines. The passages I read aloud unnerved me—launched me into hemming and

hawing, into circumlocutions leading nowhere, finally into muteness—
because Kafka's words had not left me indifferent. They mattered. They
had spoken to me. Otherwise, I would not have felt pressed to respond.
Otherwise, my response could not have been seen as wanting.

FEELING THE PULSE OF THE TEXT

I used to think that my mishap was worth recounting because of its
oddity, but now I recognize that it testifies to something that is essential
to any criticism worth doing—what I am calling poetic criticism—
something that, though everyone knows it, remains elusive. It happens all the time: I read a line from a book, reread it, examine its parts
and their workings, put it back together well enough to speak or write
about it, and yet remain a stranger to it. I go through the motions of
responding even though it has not spoken to me. And not lines alone:
sometimes I have things to say about passages and whole books and
still feel that something is missing, even amiss, between us.

For example: I read a scholar (a critic, a philosopher) whom everyone is quoting. The ideas are engaging and the path of thinking worth
following. I would like to be friends with these thoughts, jot them
down and take them home. But soon something gets in our way, and
it is difficult to say what. If I were put on the spot, I would set about
dissecting the tissue of assertions and conclusions. But is that it?

What gets in the way is linked to these, but it is more primordial,
more obscure. Before I have formed an impression of the claims and
ideas that are officially at stake, a faint dissatisfaction takes hold, an
awkwardness that grows more fraught as the minutes and pages go
by. I press on, rally my attention and do my best to like what I read,
but it is no use. Like a child, my mind wanders the minute I take my
eyes off it. I look at email. I check the news. Bit by bit I turn against
the work, and because I do not know how to put my discontent into
words, I mutter something about arguments being flawed and assump-
tions compromised.

But the reason I am restless lies elsewhere. It is closer to hand and
therefore harder to name. It is not that what I read is lifeless, but that
I cannot get close enough to feel its flesh, its pulse. It is as though the
written words and I were separated by thick panes of glass, forced to
communicate through a phone, the way visitors and inmates talk in the

movies. I see the words and hear them clearly, clearly enough to believe I understand them. But then I realize with a start that everything about seeing and hearing, everything about understanding, has changed now that the words and I do not touch.

When I set aside what I say "in public," in my "professional capacity," and look for those works that have afforded moments of intimacy, I become aware of how few they number. That does not mean that I scorn the rest, but an air of aloofness hangs over my relationship to them. Yes, the writing is deft and insightful (which is not nothing—far from it), yet it rarely comes back to me when I am lost in another task. It does not send tremors of joy or bewilderment or envy through my system, as things do that get under my skin. It does not make me put down the book and tell you about it. It does not speak to me in a way that makes me speak.

Most of the criticism and philosophy that I read does not do these things, nor does most of the literature, including most of the works that by consensus are called "great" and that I have agreed to call "great." I do not recall many moments of bliss or wounding, those moments that flare up when intimacy with a work has been achieved, while reading Jane Austen or Thomas Mann or even Shakespeare. Admiration, yes; pleasure, too, can be part of the experience, though it is usually the cold pleasure of appreciation. But intimacy? Intimacy feels different.

Putting this down can help me take a step in the right direction, for in noticing and naming this disappointment—this twinge of sadness at remaining aloof from what should touch me—at least I admit to feeling something, which is more than I permit myself in the professional spheres I inhabit. It is a modest feeling, just the vague sense of having been wrongfooted, but even so it gives expression to a longing to feel the vitality of poetic works—works of art and of reflection—a longing to encounter words or images or gestures so forceful that they seize me by the collar and shake me out of my slumber. By poetic works I mean not those that sit on the "poetry" shelf of the bookstore, nor verbal works of art in general, nor even all works of art, but works that *do* something to me (speak to me, matter to me) and, in turn, incite me to do something that matters.

The disappointment at failing to hear the poetry in a work is the photo negative of what I really seek, namely, the intimacy that must be in place if the work is to release its poetic force, if it is to crack open ways of being that have been hardened by inattention and habit—ways of perceiving, ways of thinking, and ways of doing. Intimacy may be dormant, but that just means that it can be roused.

What is this intimacy? Is it a form of attachment, an attitude, an ethos, a mood? It will take time to get to know this phenomenon well enough to open it to reflection. But since misunderstandings are likely taking root even as we speak, it may help to say what it is not: intimacy is not love (definitely not the full-blown love of romance), nor is it affinity, rapport, tenderness, sex, or a form of symbiotic union. Often it is present in these ways of being, but not always: there can be sex without intimacy; there can be tenderness without intimacy; there can even be love without intimacy—when, for example, it happens at first sight, not having waited for intimacy to arrive.

There is, then, a gap between intimacy and euphoric feelings and actions, a gap that widens when we remember that intimacy can also be active in their opposite numbers. Does hatred not burn hotter when there is intimacy between foes? Does violence not become more savage? Even mild sorrows cut more deeply. What hurts more: being snubbed by a friend or by a stranger?

The idea of intimacy tends to arrive with a surplus of warmth and benevolence, yet the truth is that its affective arrow can point down as well as up. Intimacy does not unlock the mystery of the other and open her or him or it to full comprehension: in intimacy, I can misunderstand as much as I can understand. Or, what is more unsettling, I fail to understand, not the way a sign in a language I don't know withholds its meaning, but the way the behavior of a sibling or a neighbor or a book I think I know can suddenly plunge me into the vertigo of incomprehension. To decode the sign, all I need is a dictionary or the right app. But intimacy sharpens the edge of understanding *and* its malfunctions: *both* matter more.

Intimacy, then, is not the same as closeness, and its opposite is not distance but detachment. At bottom, its way of being is participatory.

SOME EXAMPLES

What kind of writing speaks about literature, about art and film and ideas—about anything significant really—in a way that testifies to the writer's having been spoken to? What bespeaks an intimacy with the things it speaks about? For me, the answer begins not with schools or theories but with names, where names stand for titles, and titles for works, and works finally for passages or phrases or even single words that, for reasons to be explored but perhaps never understood, seem to hold a special power.

Begin at the beginning, with, for example, Erich Auerbach on Abraham's foiled sacrifice of his son:

> God gives his command, and the story itself begins: everyone knows it; it unrolls with no episodes in a few independent sentences whose syntactical connection is of the most rudimentary sort. In this atmosphere it is unthinkable that an implement, a landscape through which the travelers passed, the serving-men, or the ass, should be described, that their origin or descent or material or appearance or usefulness should be set forth in terms of praise; they do not even admit an adjective: they are serving-men, ass, wood, and knife, and nothing else, without an epithet; they are there to serve the end which God has commanded; what in other respects they were, are, or will be, remains in darkness.[1]

Or, for example, James Baldwin:

> In *Uncle Tom's Cabin*, that cornerstone of American social protest fiction, St. Clare, the kindly master, remarks to his coldly disapproving Yankee cousin, Miss Ophelia, that, so far as he is able to tell, the blacks have been turned over to the devil for the benefit of the whites in this world—however, he adds thoughtfully, it may turn out in the next. Miss Ophelia's reaction is, at least, vehemently right-minded: "This is perfectly horrible!" she exclaims. "You ought to be ashamed of yourselves!" . . . Neither of them questions the medieval morality from which their dialogue springs: black, white, the devil, the next world—posing its alternatives between heaven and the flames—were realities for them as, of course, they were for their creator. They spurned and were terrified of the darkness, striving mightily for the light; and considered from this aspect, Miss Ophelia's exclamation, like Mrs. Stowe's novel, achieves a bright, almost a lurid significance, like the light from a fire which consumes a witch.[2]

Or Roland Barthes:

> Japanese rawness is essentially visual; it denotes a certain colored state of the flesh or vegetable substance (it being understood that color is

never exhausted by a catalogue of tints, but refers to a whole tactility of substance; thus *sashimi* exhibits not so much colors as resistances: those which vary the flesh of raw fish, causing it to pass, from one end of the tray to the other, through the stations of the soggy, the fibrous, the elastic, the compact, the rough, the slippery). Entirely visual . . . , food thereby says that it is not *deep*: the edible substance is without a precious heart, without a buried power, without a vital secret: no Japanese dish is endowed with a *center* . . . ; here everything is the ornament of another ornament: first of all because on the table, on the tray, food is never anything but a collection of fragments, none of which appears privileged by an order of ingestion; to eat is not to respect a menu (an itinerary of dishes), but to select, with a light touch of the chopsticks, sometimes one color, sometimes another, depending on a kind of inspiration which appears in its slowness as the detached, indirect accompaniment of the conversation (which itself may be extremely silent).[3]

Or Kenneth Burke on *Othello*:

The work thus parallels what we have elsewhere cited a sociologist as terming a "ritual of riddance." It is a requiem in which we participate at the ceremonious death of a portion of ourselves. And whatever discomforts we may have experienced under the sway of this tension in life itself, as thus "imitated" in art it permits us the great privilege of being present at our own funeral. For though we be lowly and humiliated, we can tell ourselves at least that, as a corpse, if the usual rituals are abided by, we are assured of an ultimate dignity, that all men must pay us tribute insofar as they act properly, and that a sermon doing the best possible by us is in order.[4]

Or the final lines of Michel Foucault's essay on *Las Meninas*:

Perhaps there exists, in this painting by Velázquez, the representation, as it were, of Classical representation, and the definition of the space it opens up to us. And, indeed, representation undertakes to represent itself here in all its elements, with its images, the eyes to which it is offered, the faces it makes visible, the gestures that call it into being. But there, in the midst of this dispersion which it is simultaneously grouping together and spreading out before us, indicated compellingly from every side, is an essential void: the necessary disappearance of that which is its foundation—of the person it resembles and the person in whose eyes it is only a resemblance. This very subject—which is the same—has been elided. And representation, freed finally from the relation that was impeding it, can offer itself as representation in its pure form.[5]

Or Pauline Kael on Martin Scorsese's *Goodfellows*:

Is it a great movie? I don't think so. But it's a triumphant piece of filmmaking—journalism presented with the brio of drama. Every frame is active and vivid, and you can feel the director's passionate delight in making these pictures move. When Henry Hill (Ray Liotta), the central character, crosses a Long Island street to beat up the man who tried to put the make on his girl, the dogwood is in bloom, and all through this movie we're aware of the ultra-greenness of the suburbs that the gangsters live in; these thieves are always negotiating their way through shrubs and hedges.[6]

Or, last instance, Susan Sontag:

It should be noted that interpretation is not simply the compliment that mediocrity pays to genius. It is, indeed, the modern way of understanding something, and is applied to works of every quality. Thus, in the notes that Elia Kazan published on his production of *A Streetcar Named Desire*, it becomes clear that, in order to direct the play, Kazan had to discover that Stanley Kowalski represented the sensual and vengeful barbarism that was engulfing our culture, while Blanche Du Bois was Western civilization, poetry, delicate apparel, dim lighting, refined feelings and all, though a little the worse for wear to be sure. Tennessee Williams' forceful psychological melodrama now became intelligible: it was *about* something, about the decline of Western civilization. Apparently, were it to go on being a play about a handsome brute named Stanley Kowalski and a faded mangy belle named Blanche Du Bois, it would not be manageable.[7]

I admit this is a motley assortment. Between these passages there is hardly an overlap in concepts, themes, or aims. Given how much energy I have put into tangling with and untangling theories, it is confusing—no: it is embarrassing—that a critic's theoretical commitments seem to do exactly *nothing* to predict whether I end up finding his or her work engaging. (I have found that the same goes for philosophers.) Those commitments also fail to predict why over time some works migrate from engaging to indifferent and vice versa.

What, then, is it that draws me to these passages? The same things that I suppose might draw anyone: seeing something I had not seen before, not in *that* way; humor; lucidity; cheek; fierce thinking. Yet, more than anything, it is to be exposed to the courage—the *daring*—in a piece of writing and to be seized and infected by it. It is to be struck by the blazing recognition that I did not know you were *allowed* to say that. I did not know you could call *Othello* "a requiem in which we participate at the ceremonious death of a portion of ourselves." I did not know that a novel's significance could be described as being "like the light from a fire which consumes a witch." To the best of my knowledge, I have not participated at a requiem for the death of a portion of myself, nor have I witnessed the fire consuming a witch, yet these impossible images, apart from whatever they say about *Othello* and *Uncle Tom's Cabin*, hold within themselves the power to allow *me* to speak.

By taking liberties, these passages grant me liberty. By having the boldness to speak, they let me speak more boldly. (That I squander the chance is not their failing.) When I feel stuck lining up words on a page, I open a volume by Nietzsche or Baldwin, more or less at random, and wait for some of the electricity coursing through their words to leap over to mine. How crude, you might say, how instrumental. In fact, I know of no greater compliment one can pay a work: crediting it with the power of arousing the urge of making. If poetic making—hence also poetic criticism—has an essential mark, it is this: an infectious productivity.

What draws me, then, to writings such as the ones I quoted is their poetic urgency, which they generate by being drawn, in turn, to works that speak to them (works like Genesis, *Goodfellows*, and sushi). The writers' motivations vary: they may be animated by philological scruples, they may be itching for a fight or reaching for a tone just this side of snark: yet in every case what they write about matters to them. Which is how and why it can come to matter to me. An intimacy that links *them* to things comes to tie me to them, to the things they write of but also to the writing itself. Their intimacy becomes my intimacy.

My list of quotes, then, is perhaps less of a hodgepodge than I've made it sound. The writers may not stand in direct lines of filiation nor share an intellectual temperament, yet anyone who has read even a few pages of their writings will be struck by a vivid affinity drawing them together. It expresses itself first in what they *fail* to do: They do not "do research" that, down the line, finds its documentation in words. They do not write down (or write up) what they know already. They write, rather, to free themselves of up and down (of right and left, and even of right and wrong). They write to lose their way and lose, too, some of the knowledge that guides them and weighs on them—lose, therefore, something of themselves—before coming upon a mode of thinking and feeling that discloses the world in a new way. (Or not: once you have lost your way, you never know what you may come upon.) They write "about" this or that, but mainly they write, period. Their writing is not the final resting place for research but the workshop where they work out the shape and weight and texture of ideas.

POETIC CRITICISM, AN ESSAY

Am I saying that one thing these passages share, one thing that unites the miscellany of themes and moods, is belonging to the genre of the essay? Much speaks for it. Do the names of their authors not appear on essays and essay collections? Are they not essayists? And essayists write essays, do they not. Perhaps the true home of criticism worth writing—of poetic criticism—is not this theory or that, nor this method or that, but the essay.

That seems right, provided we handle "essay" correctly. We tend to think it is a genre: essays are gathered in volumes and placed on shelves labeled "essays"; courses are taught on the essay. But what makes an essay an essay is also what disqualifies it from being a genre. It is not a thing endowed with well-defined dimensions and features, which is why the aim in writing an essay cannot be to end up with "an essay." The life of the essay does not lie in a noun.

Where then? In a verb? That draws closer to the mark: *essay*, lexicographers tell us, derives from the Middle French verb *essayer*. The essay is not a thing but a way of doing, a form of action, and a strange sort of action at that. For "to essay"—"to attempt," "to experiment"—is not an action with a fixed set of attributes that can be placed alongside other actions such as "to dance," "to cook," or "to write." "To essay" is not to do something specific but to do anything at all, yet *differently*. It names a second-order action, a way of acting on other actions: when I essay, then I dance, cook, or write, but in a particular way, namely experimentally. I do not write an essay, nor do I essay to write, but I write essayistically.

So, the heart of the essay beats in the adverb, which is less strange than it may sound. Is that not the norm among phenomena that interest us here? Is it not true, for example, of poetry? The essence of poetry lies not in manufacturing a product that falls into a category labeled "poetry," but in making anything at all—but poetically. (I have no more than an inkling of the difference that doing something "poetically" makes, but might know more by the end of this book.) The same holds for "play," which is not limited to a range of acts and behaviors definable once and for all, for I can do anything playfully. To be sure, these mode of doing are not the same, though they do maintain an intimacy with one another, as they do with intimacy itself. Intimacy develops essaystically, poetically, and playfully. The same can be said of poetic criticism. It is adverbial: not a thing, but a manner of making.

ROLAND BARTHES HAS SUSHI

Earlier, seeking to inch closer to the intimacy that prevails when I hear something speak to me, I gave some examples. That gesture assumed that intimacy is the kind of thing susceptible to disclosing itself in examples. Is it? Did it? Did I manage to show you something speaking to me by quoting it? Or did I simply repeat what I did in class when I read aloud Kafka's words, banking on their magical power of being their own explanation? Let's be generous to ourselves and call this a "strategy": does it work? Is it able to register and to convey—to feel and to pass on—the power that reaches out from the past to seize the present? Sometimes it is, yes; sometimes all you need to say—all you *can* say—about a phrase is to quote it, the way a name, in its very nakedness, can be the most eloquent epitaph.

But sometimes not: sometimes more needs to be said, not only because (as writing tutors insist) your reader needs more to see and to feel what you mean, but also because *you* need more to know what you mean. It is less a question of deciphering—of interpreting—what the voice speaking to you has said than of figuring out what you are to do about it. What does it want you to say or do? Did you hear right, or were you imagining the solicitation? In rallying your resources to face these questions, you undergo a process of becoming the kind of being capable of hearing the call in Kafka's words, or Baldwin's or Kael's or Sontag's. That is what criticism is good for: in telling the other why something bowled you over, not only do you afford yourself a chance to discover why. You transform yourself such that you *can be* bowled over.

Each of the passages I offered could become the occasion for this sort of exploratory, probing writing—for an essay—that incites a change in the possibilities of experience, a change in the reader but, above all, in the writer. Take one of the examples, which, while not chosen at random, is also not offered as the exemplar of exemplars; it is, rather, one of many possible points of departure leading, perhaps, to different paths and different books. Barthes's passage comes from his book about Japan, *Empire of Signs*, where over many pages devoted to Japanese food, he . . . well, what exactly does he do with and to the food? Let's have another look:

Japanese rawness is essentially visual; it denotes a certain colored state of the flesh or vegetable substance (it being understood that color is never exhausted by a catalogue of tints, but refers to a whole tactility of substance; thus *sashimi* exhibits not so much colors as resistances: those which vary the flesh of raw fish, causing it to pass, from one end of the tray to the other, through the stations of the soggy, the fibrous, the elastic, the compact, the rough, the slippery). Entirely visual . . . , food thereby says that it is not *deep*: the edible substance is without a precious heart, without a buried power, without a vital secret: no Japanese dish is endowed with a *center* . . . ; here everything is the orna-ment of another ornament: first of all because on the table, on the tray, food is never anything but a collection of fragments, none of which appears privileged by an order of ingestion; to eat is not to respect a menu (an itinerary of dishes), but to select, with a light touch of the chopsticks, sometimes one color, sometimes another, depending on a kind of inspiration which appears in its slowness as the detached, indirect accompaniment of the conversation (which itself may be ex-tremely silent).

A strange passage in a strange book. Does it provide a description? It does, and in detail, but not to lend a hand. To someone who has not had a Japanese meal, it fails to provide even a basic map, and someone who has may be puzzled to find this arrangement of indeterminate substances in place of the familiar order of sushi. Yet the description is not therefore merely bewildering. Rather, it hides from view the outlines of what I know—or *think* I know—and with a magician's gesture reveals . . . the same object once again. But now the object looks different and more interesting, the way an ordinary pebble looks like a precious stone when presented in a small white box. The description works a bit like a still life: what it shows belongs to the everyday, and yet I have never seen it quite like *that*. In fact, I now get the feeling that, though I have encountered it a hundred times, I have never really *seen* sushi, never really *looked* at its glossy finish or the eerie springiness of its flesh, which rests on a knife's edge dividing the appetizing from the disgusting.

Is the passage an interpretation, then? Clearly, Barthes has a take on Japanese food, yet he does not seek to uncover the true meaning concealed in the plate of sashimi, if that is what we mean by interpretation. His way of interpreting has much in common with his way of describing: rather than lifting a veil to disclose a hidden truth, it lifts a veil to disclose what I see and feel and taste already, or what I could have been seeing and feeling and tasting, had I only been attentive the way Barthes is. It is the description of the texture of flesh that reveals the mystery of its colors, which in turn discloses the recognition that the truth of this flesh lies in itself, not in an unseen depth.

WHAT DOES THE TEXT WANT FROM ME?

Rather than asking what the passage on sushi does, we might turn the tables and ask what it wants me to do: how does it wish to be read, heard, spoken about? In literary studies, as in other academic disciplines, we are primed to identify a thesis and evaluate the evidence marshaled in its favor. Here, the thesis might roughly look like this:

> Japanese food is arranged like an abstract tableau of colors and textures, anchored by no central motif, from which the diner, using chopsticks instead of a brush, removes now this, now that element, unpainting the painting while eating.

It is a compelling thesis, sharp enough to call me into action right away (to doubt, defend, improve, or dismiss it), but is it how the passage wishes to be read? Is that the experience Barthes's work aims to awaken if its idea is to take root in my consciousness? Is it the comportment that this work teaches? Manifestly it is not. Only someone with a tin ear would convert the passage into a chain of syllogisms and think nothing of it.

Boiling the passage down to a thesis shortchanges not only the text but also my experience of it, for it deprives me of feeling on my tongue the texture of language, which, in turn, discloses the texture of Japanese food. If there is truth in the passage, it reveals itself not in propositions but in the grain of the adjectives, in the cadence of its sentences, in resonances with other passages in the book (and other books).

The first thing that Barthes's passage wishes me to do, then, is to hear its call, which means becoming vulnerable to its significance. That is what intimacy signifies: I do not take the posture of the detached observer but maintain an attachment even before I have set about analyzing and interpreting. This is not an attitude specific to literature or art: speaking to the students in his Introduction to Philosophy lecture course, Martin Heidegger insisted that any sort of understanding is sustained by an "inner friendship with the things themselves":

> Understanding needs a special and constant effort that from the beginning must be supported by a primordial inclination to the things. This inclination, this inner friendship with the things themselves, is what is called *philia*—a friendship that, like every real friendship, following its essence fights for what it loves.[8]

Philia nourishes *philosophia*, and not it alone; *philologia*, too, relies on *philia*. Without it, there is no understanding, there is no hearing and no speaking.

But this friendship, like every real friendship, bears risks. Inclination makes me partial to the things I face—makes me *face* what I face—and in so doing, it can perturb my equilibrium: *Neigung*—Heidegger's term—means both "inclination" and "an incline," both "fondness" and "slope" or "gradient." What I love can trip me up: it can make me speak or sing, or lead me to stutter. But those who have loved know that already.

I imagine this talk of fondness and friendship makes some readers squirm. *Surely* I am not suggesting that I take novels and paintings to act like people. We scholars, we critics and philosophers, have long castigated the fallacy—the *sin*—of anthropomorphism, insisting on the material and historical differences between persons and objects. Fine. But nothing about the relationship to poetic works of any kind (of art, philosophy, reflection, and the rest) would get off the ground if we did *not* give them a human shape and a human voice. Here, the poetic thinker Stanley Cavell is my witness. About objects of art, he has written:

> We are not merely involved with them, but concerned with them, and care about them; we treat them in special ways, invest them with a value which normal people otherwise reserve only for other people— *and* with the same kind of scorn and outrage. They *mean* something to us, not just the way statements do, but the way people do. . . . The category of intention is as inescapable (or escapable with the same consequences) in speaking of objects of art as in speaking of what human beings say and do: without it, we would not understand what they are.[9]

Cavell is not suggesting that people and artworks intend in exactly the same way or must be treated equally under all conditions, just that people's comportment toward works of art—toward any poetic works, I would say—would make no sense if we prohibited thinking of works as entities that speak to me and that I am called to respond to, if we renounced the language of inclination or care or outrage—the language of intimacy.

What does an intimacy with the passage from Barthes give me? The ability to understand, but certainly not full comprehension, much less agreement. It gives me something else, both less than comprehension and more. Intimacy allows me to hear the accent in Barthes's thinking, not merely in the words he has chosen but in the consistency of the things themselves—the elasticity of the fish and the finish of the vegetables. It lets me feel the way tactility and visuality vie for attention in his essay. That does not mean that I will always take pleasure in the passage. On some days, I might find it precious and overwritten. But even then I engage not with a thesis or a logical construction stripped of all flesh.

If I find intimacy with the passage, then I see not merely a tray of sushi but a tray conjured by someone with a carnal existence: this is not the abstraction we call a "writer" (as I am no "reader") but someone with a front and a back, a history and a future. I need not check the title page to realize that the passage was written by someone with a proper name: every phrase tells me that a specific someone called Roland Barthes put down these words, in a particular situation, in a place and time identified not by geometric coordinates but through a network of reminiscences, ambitions, moods, fears, wishes, and intentions. In the grain of this human being's voice I feel passions, even when they fail to surface. Though there is neither the word "I" nor an autobiographical fact to be found in the passage, this is a voice with a body, with arms and legs, and something between the legs.

But we are also distant—even more distant than we are from disembodied observation—from an autobiographically authenticated "personal" account. Look at the passage. Every word bears Barthes's stamp, yet there is not a personal trace, not a hint of whether the meal was satisfying or the company pleasant. The passage is saturated with appetites, though not with the appetites of a specific body—Roland Barthes's—nor with an appetite for *this* meal. (I confess that reading the passage and the pages around it invariably arouses a craving for sushi in me, so much so that sometimes I seek it out before going to a Japanese restaurant. Do I abuse the text when I use it as an aphrodisiac?) Autobiography has not been banished: when I read the book, I cannot help thinking that a man named Roland Barthes did, in fact, spend time in Japan, time that included visits to restaurants. Yet the singularity of the account does not rely on the authenticating power of the first-person experience.

Instead, we become witness to how the quotidian particularity of a life, once it vibrates with poetry, goes beyond itself, not by bracketing the particular but by intensifying it. Barthes describes exactly this process when he considers how Marcel Proust fashions the "I" of *In Search of Lost Time*:

> The Proustian oeuvre brings on stage (or into writing) an "I" (the Narrator); but this "I," one may say, is not quite a self (subject and object of traditional autobiography): "I" is not the one who remembers, confides, confesses, he is the one who discourses; the person this "I" brings on stage is a writing self whose links with the self of civil life are uncertain, displaced. . . . It is vain to wonder if the book's Narrator is

Proust (in the civil meaning of the patronymic): it is simply another
Proust, often unknown to himself.[10]

Just the same way, the voice we hear is that of a displaced Barthes. And
only because this other Barthes is often unknown to himself can he
transmute idiosyncrasy into universality. The specificity of *his* sashimi
is what discloses its essence to us. His signature, singular like every
signature, becomes the mark of a general significance.

THE IMPERSONALITY OF INTIMACY

An "I" that is not quite a self, an "I" often unknown to itself—that "I"
is essential to poetic criticism, as it is essential to every poetic making.
Why essential? For one, because intimacy can be felt only by an "I";
it can only become meaningful to an "I." Only I can be elated or shat-
tered in intimacy. It is true that it is possible to speak of a generalized
intimacy, just as it is possible to speak about friendship or love or death
in abstractions; it is done all the time.

The problem with this way of speaking is that, in remaining blind to
the singular instance, it sees too much and too clearly; it grasps its phenomenon too firmly and completely. Friendship as such has features
one can enumerate; love as such has a history one can tell; the shape of
death as such can become the object of medical and legal scrutiny. But
friendship and love and death can be understood as the bewildering
phenomena they are only if I have had and lost a friend, if I have had
my heart broken, if I have faced the paralysis that the idea of my own
death brings about. Which is why Barthes seeks this "I" that is more
than it knows against the diluted "we" of a science of poetry:

> I shall be speaking of "myself." "Myself" is to be understood here in
> the full sense: not the asepticized substitute of a general reader (any
> substitution is an asepsis); I shall be speaking of the one for whom no
> one else can be substituted, for better and for worse. It is the intimate
> which seeks utterance in me, seeks to make its cry heard, confronting
> generality, confronting science.[11]

As this "I" exceeds the abstracted "we" of a generalized discourse, it
also declines to submerge itself in its personal particularities and social

identities (which amount to another sort of particularity, one collective and collectivized). Which is why "I" and "myself" appear in scare quotes: the "I" of poetic criticism is not the I of quotidian life, the entity known to others and the one with which I maintain familiarity. It is the I unknown to myself, the I that exceeds not just generality but also particularity, exceeds it through the vibrancy of making.

That means that "the intimate which seeks utterance in me," this intimacy that prevails between me and the thing that calls to me, is not a personal matter. It has something impersonal, something public, about it, something that remains opaque to the I itself.

That is a powerful thought, but it is also a strange thought, not easy to inhabit. I tend to experience whatever kind of intimacy I have (or fail to have) with a person or a place or a line from a book as a matter between the two of us, the result of a history involving us, and us alone. But saying that this intimacy, because it activates an "I" that is a stranger to itself, involves what is impersonal in me, means that this history of ours is not and cannot be an island detached from other histories. It is not a matter of private commerce but is pushed and pulled by the undertows of capital-H History in which we find ourselves. Intimacy is haunted by History and in turn haunts it. Though it fails to determine me, a historical and social ecology not of my choosing gives shape to my movements: religions, political orders, scientific systems, languages, and social arrangements make part of this history. Intimacy—intact or damaged, threadbare or textured—emerges in these crosscurrents, is shaped by them, and in turn shapes them.

THE TEXTURE OF INTIMACY

If I feel an intimacy developing with Barthes's writing, where do I find its source? Not in a textual location for which I could give chapter and verse, just as little as a foul mood shows up in a brain scan. This is true not only of my encounters with poetic works; it is true of experience generally. Gestalt psychology and phenomenology have long taught that in experience I face not naked objects that I then, in a second step, wrap in layers of emotional and conceptual significance. My encounter does not begin with facts that dwell in a zone of detachment called "objectivity," only to become "subjective" once they come into contact with my body and my history. Rather, from the start, the things of my world stand in relation to me, one way or the other. They arrive saturated by meanings and feelings. They have significance.

Kurt Koffka, a founder of Gestalt psychology, devoted his career to demonstrating the pervasiveness of affect and meaning in experience. "An object looks attractive or repulsive before it looks black or blue, circular or square," he claims.[12] You can quibble about whether affective judgments do indeed precede cognitive judgments, whether being attractive or repulsive must always come "before" being black or blue. What matters is that every blue I experience cannot help but be caught in the magnetic field of attraction and repulsion that courses between the blue thing and me (a field haunted by history and politics). The untouched blue, the blue of chromatic scales and color wheels, the objective blue registered by the instruments of physics—that blue is not the starting point of experience but arrives at the end of an elaborate process of abstraction. And even then, one wonders how aloof from feeling and significance this abstracted blue manages to remain. Look at Gerhard Richter's paintings of the color chart: their abstraction is as rigorous as can be, yet their beauty reveals just how fragile this abstraction is, how difficult it is to keep it from sliding into significance.

Maurice Merleau-Ponty, whose phenomenology of perception seeks to be attuned to Gestalt psychology, thinks empiricism is flawed because it gets perception backward: it starts by isolating the basic units of sensation—blue and black, circular and square—then constructs experience by joining one to the other like Tinkertoys. But that, he insists, yields an account of the world denuded precisely of what characterizes perception:

> Empiricism excludes from perception the anger or the pain which I nevertheless read in a face, the religion whose essence I seize in some hesitation or reticence, the city whose temper I recognize in the attitude of a policeman or the style of a public building.[13]

Empiricism excludes from the world what, finally, makes a world. It opens its eyes and ears, but rather than taking in things as they present themselves, it fixes on objects with the aim of taking their measure, all the while remaining deaf and blind to the intimacy that pervades their every fold.

Earlier, I described the pang of unease that can settle over experience when I cannot find intimacy with a work. Now we come across a way of describing things, a way common in science, that works to banish intimacy altogether. In both, intimacy remains absent. But between these two absences there is a world of difference. In the one, the elusiveness of intimacy leaves its imprint on the experience and shapes it just as a fully unfolded intimacy would. In the other, the absence of intimacy is the point. The first is sensitive to a lack; the second lacks sensitivity.

That is why intimacy is not a mere feature of experience but one of its dimensions. It colors experience not only when it is in full bloom but also when stunted. An unrealized friendship with a person or a work can be as significant as a fully realized one; my disappointment at a failed intimacy pervades my thoughts and actions no less than does the joy of a flourishing one. If a person or thing is to have significance for me, then I cannot simply subtract the dimension of intimacy from experience. I cannot dwell in a state of inert neutrality toward this person or thing, as science requires. Rather, my experience remains in motion, always leaping forward or falling back along the axis of intimacy: anticipating what it might become, enjoying its familiarity, dreading its retreat, longing for its revival, mourning its demise.

That poetic works do not lend themselves to being grasped and held up for inspection like the objects of science does not mean that they are lost to vagueness and unreality; we feel them and recognize them with all the vividness of anything whose coordinates we can name— often with more sharpness and more intensity. It just means that the direct gaze will not disclose the truth of intimacy (nor that of mood or flair or sashimi).

We know why indirection is required here. I never *have* intimacy— with a passage, an image, a person, a dwelling—once and for all, the way I lay claim to my possessions. I *know* intimacy when I have it, but this is not a piece of selfsame knowledge to which I can hold fast, to be amended and shared as needed; I have it as much, and as little, as I have the experience, but I do not own it.

This makes us aware of how strangely entangled solidity and fragility are in intimacy: so utterly felt is this way of relating to the world that it remains unperturbed by skeptical agitation. Because it is not an articulated system of beliefs, its texture, smooth and dense, offers no cracks through which doubts could seep. When there is intimacy with a work or a person, a room or a house, nothing seems capable of breaking the bond. The feeling recedes into an obscure depth, almost out of reach of consciousness, where, rather than itself being experienced, it becomes the stage for experience, akin to what Martin Heidegger means by "being-in-the-world."

Yet at every moment, this mode of existence, so calming in its weight, is at risk of crumbling. A false note, a maladroit gesture—anything jarring—can bring it to ruin and leave me alone with my disappointment. What makes this loss more painful still is that I never know, and perhaps never *can* know, where the dissonance comes from. Was it the other—a friend, or else a dancer on stage, the narrator of a novel, the movie camera lingering on a face, or a few lines about sushi—was it this other who paused too long, or not long enough, leaving me adrift? Or was it me—my fear and my need for reassurance? Who spoiled this delicious intimacy we had? We could argue, and we do, but only because we know it does not matter: the damage is done.

That means: if intimacy can be lost, it can be gained; it can be developed and achieved. Because we fail to come up with a recipe for bringing it about, we let ourselves think it falls from the sky. But we know it is made: I meet a friend or play Art Pepper or open *Empire of Signs*, and within a few beats—there it is. Not always, but often enough.

PRODUCTIVE DISTRUST

Intimacy can be gained, I have said. I can learn to hear the call that prompts a response. But how? This is not something I learned in school, nor do I know how to teach it. It's important that I find a way, for when intimacy remains out of reach, I face not art and reflection but their zombie twins. These signs speak and move like the real things; I can parse them and spell out the logic that propels them. But their meanings are ghost meanings. They exist on the far side of the glass wall in the prison visiting room, where everything looks and sounds familiar, but nothing is in fact the same.

Mad as it might sound, that is the canonical posture recommended by all disciplines that pursue the scholarly—the *wissenschaftlich*—study of poetic works. Detachment is what I learned and is what I teach, for the simple reason that blocking intimacy can be a most generative act. The literary scholar Paul de Man knows this as well as anyone. "A mood of distrust," he writes, "produces rather than paralyzes interpretive discourse."[14]

Distrust is a mighty deity: it destroys, and, in destroying, it creates. It puts an end to guileless reading and in its stead fuels the production of "interpretive discourse." The two powers of distrust work like the two ends of a seesaw: as guileless reading is driven into the ground, interpretation rises to greater heights. But the new systems of meaning produced by distrust themselves fall prey to the corrosive power of distrust, and so the anxious manufacture of interpretive discourse goes on and on, without end. That, in a nutshell, is what the interpretive disciplines do, and it is why Distrust is their muse. De Man's work is peerless for the skill and ruthlessness with which it unleashes both powers of distrust, the destructive and the constructive, yet the moves are by no means his alone; even novices learn to make them.

If distrust "produces rather than paralyzes interpretive discourse," that does not mean that overcoming distrust results in paralysis or muteness. The idea is not to stop speaking but to stop producing "interpretive discourse"—to stop interpreting by "running to and fro" (which is just what *discursus* means). It is to put an end to the hustle and bustle of meaning making. But the end of interpretive discourse is not the end of interpretation or of criticism, nor is intimacy their nemesis. In fact, it is the setting in which true interpretation unfolds and the source from which it draws its force.

To learn the intimacy that leads me to poetic criticism, should I then sidestep distrust altogether? Should I abandon the procedures I have spent years honing and set aside scholarship, critique, and other techniques of detachment? That is what some writers urge whose work has been labeled "postcritical": to choose love and attachment over suspicion, to aim for reparative reading over paranoid reading.[15] And it is true that intimacy finds a home in the ways of perceiving and understanding that remain untroubled by suspicion: the "naïve reader," whom scholars and critics unite in disparaging, is at least not barricaded behind concepts and methods. This reader remains capable of feeling (delight, surprise, boredom) and of admitting to those feelings. That's something. But it's not enough—or rather, it is too much.

There are modes of intimacy that promise more than they can

keep. They activate feelings—of empathy, kinship, solidarity, even symbiosis—that lead me to believe that the person or the book before me is not holding anything back. The other is now transparent to me. I understand him or her or it completely. Rather than laboring over words and phrases, all I need to do is look deeply enough into the other's eyes. Or I follow the suggestion of Goethe's *Elective Affinities* and open the small window installed in the other's forehead to glimpse the thoughts that have yet to be uttered. Words are no longer stumbling blocks to understanding but melt into instant, fluent comprehension.

But that way lies delusion, the delusion of telepathic comprehension, and puncturing this delusion has been the mission of the interpretive disciplines. Nothing puts Paul de Man on edge like the scent of "the seductive powers of identification" in a work of literature.[16] Nothing makes him more vigilant than a text that flatters its reader into complicity. Which is why when approaching a poet like Rilke, who has a knack for seducing readers into sincere fellow feeling, de Man arrives with all the instruments of distrust that philology has to offer. He assures us that, thus armed, "it is not difficult . . . to demystify this seduction" and elude the trap of an "intersubjective reading grounded in a common sentiment, in the 'transparency of the heart'" (21). Now he can move into the text with confidence, for a man of science is not easily seduced.

LEARNING TO UNLEARN

Where does that leave intimacy? Is it just another name for giving in to "the seductive powers of identification," for complicity and mystification, for the deluded wish for a transparent heart or a window in the forehead? It is true that intimacy is not free of these modes of experience; they may even come to colonize it. But a debased form of intimacy is no cause for abandoning it altogether.

In naïve reading I develop closeness, not intimacy, and while it is the object that feels close, the closeness is mainly with myself—actually, with an image of myself. Everything mirrors my world and speaks my tongue, prodding me to find myself in what I see and hear. When I succeed, I am pleased, and when I come up empty, I declare the work incomprehensible or outdated (or "unrelatable") and set it aside, none the wiser or more foolish for it.

That way, I mostly find what I possess already. The world I encounter is so full—full mostly of images of myself—that intimacy finds no room to breathe, the way too much closeness can suffocate a friendship. I empathize with the fate of those I encounter in a story; I identify with a point of view that I discover in a philosophical reflection; I project my worries and wants; and soon the work is peopled with imaginary versions of myself, so much so that hardly any air is left for the sensitivity and knowledge that intimacy enables. Intimacy is not extinguished entirely, but it is overwhelmed by the weight of moral and intellectual vanity. Every teacher knows that unpracticed students, like prophets and child prodigies, can suddenly speak the truth, seizing on something essential in a work, something that may elude expert readers even after years of study. But as a rule, such insights are just as suddenly washed away by waves of earnestly felt solidarity or indignation or nostalgia linked to some character or theme.

If distrust is the muse of the interpretive disciplines, and if these disappoint by turning their objects into symbolic contraptions drained of life and of significance, then it makes sense no longer to call on that muse. It makes sense to drop out of the "school of suspicion" and to flout the "limits of critique,"[17] for what do suspicion and critique do but contrive cunning ways of fencing me off from the work? When I wield distrust, I become untouchable; it cloaks me in invincibility. And critique? It can work like a magic potion that renders me invulnerable to error. Since I do not set out to meet a poetic work like an enemy, I need to be stripped of this protection and released from this knowingness. So, I must forgo distrust.

Yet I also need distrust. I cannot simply take a shortcut around it, not because this or that institution (the school, the scholarly community, the "tradition") has placed it in my way. I need it to keep me from rediscovering in every novel, in every film and every essay, the psychic and social order I inhabit already. I need it to pry loose the grip that my ego has on my modes of perception and of understanding. Its sharp edge prods me to acknowledge the irreducible strangeness in art and philosophy, which leads me to acknowledge the more profound, and the more obscure, strangeness I maintain with myself. I must give up distrust and critique to be freed from the tyranny of being right, yet I need them if I am to be freed from the no less stifling tyranny of being too much with myself.

Learning to develop intimacy with a work consists, then, of *unlearn-*

ing: what I seek is not the warm bath of primordial trust but the work of leaving behind distrust. And to leave it behind, I must first hold it. It is in unburdening myself of the armory of distrust that true intimacy arrives, and not in the buoyancy of innocence. That is the source of the happiness it offers: how much sharper the bliss is in having thrown off a load than the bland feeling of never having carried one! What makes it blissful is that muscles and bones, knowing full well their ability to stem great weight, instead profligately—arrogantly—do nothing but feel themselves.

NAÏVETÉ

"Naïveté is the goal, not the origin," the philosopher Theodor Adorno has declared. "The ideal perception of artworks would be that in which what is mediated becomes immediate."[18]

When you read enough Adorno, you get lulled into the sense that you know what is coming before the text itself does. Which is why it is easy to miss how remarkable—how startling—it is to see this standard-bearer of Critical Theory, more deeply devoted to ceaseless reflection even than to his mandarin tastes, posit naïveté as the ultimate end of his undertaking. Ideally, "what is mediated becomes immediate." But let us not forget that this is Adorno. The naïveté he has in mind is not a refuge from the toils of reflection but something to be achieved *by* reflection. One arrives not at naïveté pure and simple—at naïve naïveté—but at what he calls "naïveté of a second order" (1).

As so often in Adorno, even when things sound right, you trip over the false notes. Is naïveté the right term for the state of mind that, by his own lights, should prevail in the encounter with the work of art? Is positing naïveté as the goal not a result of the rigors of dialectical thinking, which at every step insists on bringing forth the opposite of the current moment? By this way of thinking, critical reflection, taken to its end, must surely give way to its utter absence (like in the parable with which Heinrich von Kleist concludes his essay "On the Mari-onette Theater": once "knowledge has gone through the world of the infinite," human beings reclaim their graceful innocence and find the gates of Eden thrown wide open again).[19]

What makes Adorno's choice of term even odder is that no line of thinking in his aesthetic theory leads to, much less reaches, naïveté as the ideal state in which to engage artworks. Not a sentence in *Aesthetic Theory*, the book from which the quoted phrases are taken, actually displays naïveté—of the first, second, or third order. The "ideal perception of artworks" does not dialectally hopscotch between reflection and its naïve absence, nor between the "immediate" and "what is mediated." As Adorno knows better than most, the idea of immediate perception, certainly of works of art, crumbles under the slightest pressure. It's mediation all the way down.[20]

The maladroitness of these terms testifies to something worth noting, namely, to a feeling that the incessant churn of the dialectical wheel, far from favoring it, harms "the ideal perception of artworks." A melancholy scene unfolds in the book: we see Adorno aching for the stillness of naïveté and dreaming of the immediacy of perception, but only because those are the ideals that his philosophy permits him to name (while deftly keeping them at bay), when in fact he already holds in his hands what he seeks.

What *Aesthetic Theory* shows on nearly every page and on nearly every line, just as Adorno's many essays on music and literature do, is an intimacy with the works that he engages. It is intimacy, not naïveté, that permits him to ascend to the peaks of philosophical speculation, where the air is thin and the heights vertiginous, without losing touch with the singular experience that works of art entail. That is not because intimacy furnishes some pre-reflexive, nonconceptual ground that sustains reflection, a bedrock of immediacy on which reflection rests and to which it remains bound (as "the body," affect, or intuition is understood to do in theories that attempt to ground reflection on what is taken to precede it). Intimacy is not a mysterious knowing before knowing, nor a feeling that remains exempt from second thoughts. It vouches for no unassailable access to one's own feelings and thoughts. On the contrary.

In intimacy, my thoughts and feelings are put at risk in the encounter. Only in moments of intimacy can a line of writing or of music or of drawing be charged with enough significance, and with the right kind of significance, to matter to me, to elate or confound or distress me. Only then can it cause a shift in the ways I face a thing and, thus, a shift in my world and in myself. Rather than grounding and guiding what an object can mean to me, intimacy renders me vulnerable to the force of its meaning—to its significance. That, and not naïveté, is what comes through in the best moments of Adorno's writings on art.

INTIMACY, SELF-TAUGHT

The idea, then, is not to end up in naïveté, but to start with intimacy. But we are at a loss as to how to get to the starting point. It is true there is no recipe for gaining intimacy, just as little as there is a method for falling in love or becoming religious. Yet these experiences are not therefore capricious.

How to go about it then? Not by setting up a "research project" that studies the phenomenon like a specimen, but rather by finding ways of gaining intimacy with intimacy itself. Occasions for learning are many and close to hand. In fact, they present themselves in every work that makes a claim on me. They teach me how to hear them and move with them. Sometimes (for examples, reading *Empire of Signs*) things go smoothly: hardly has it shifted a foot than I welcome the step, like a dancer who gradually gets the hang of it. At other times (reading Kleist, for example, or Kafka), things can get rough: I slide and stumble along, and because the work lets go of me just when I need to be steadied, sometimes I find myself on my face.

If I am reading a book or watching a movie, then I let myself be led, which is itself an art. Since the work is new to me, I do not know what it wants from me, where I am to go and how to listen, and so I look to it for guidance. And the well-wrought work provides it. "A painter like Cézanne, an artist, or a philosopher, must not only create and express an idea, but must also awaken the experiences which will make the idea take root in the consciousness of others," Maurice Merleau-Ponty writes. "If a work is successful, it has the strange power of being self-teaching."[21] He could just as well have put the idea the other way around: if a work has the power to be self-teaching, it is successful. The artist or philosopher does not create twice, first a work and then a technique allowing the viewer or reader to take in the work. Rather, the power to create the work and the "strange power" of teaching how to encounter it are one and the same. To learn intimacy, I let the work teach me.

THE CALL OF SIGNIFICANCE

If I now return to my classroom where, clutching Kafka's *Trial*, all I can think of doing is to read passage after passage from the book, I ask myself if I have not blown this failing out of proportion. Is it so strange that my inability to comment coherently on the novel ended up leaving me unsettled and ashamed? I was a teacher speaking to students, and so my failure to tell them something—anything—worth knowing amounted to a dereliction of duty, which *should* leave me unnerved.

That is true, yet it misses the point. I have, after all, committed blunders more serious than that in the classroom, and they have not come to haunt me so. Why, then, should *this* stay with me?

Lodged in this academic setting with its fixed roles and routines, there is another scene, fluid and fragile, that is the real source of unsettlement. The fact that my speech that day was demanded—and in the end, purchased—by an institution (the university that employs me), and that my failure at producing it amounted therefore to a breach of an obligation I had assumed, veils the power of a more profound and more obscure obligation at work in this scene: the obligation to respond to the call of Kafka's words. I need to better understand this obligation to respond, for the obligation wrapped in the call is the wellspring of the urgency to act—the urgency of poetic criticism.

If this thought is to take root, we mustn't let the word "obligation" frighten us. Obligation comes in many guises: it can be folded into a demand or a command, an indebtedness, a solicitation, a request, even into a trifling flirtation. It can seize me by the neck or charm me with a wink. (Sometimes, like when reading Kafka, I get the feeling that it does both at once.) But if the speech act (or gestural act or musical act . . .) is to strike its mark, I must hear and register its claim to significance. I must become vulnerable to its call, which just means: I must allow an intimacy to take hold between us.

One way in which hearing its call manifests itself is in speech. Being called upon to speak about a book or other significant thing is therefore not an obligation that draws the greater part of its force from the classroom (or similar setting). Which is why it is not in the classroom (or similar setting) alone that *failing* to say something leaves me smarting.

I wonder: Does the work really call me, or am I hearing voices? How may I describe this call in a way that makes it seem less like a mystical experience, or even a delusion?

I said we mustn't let the word "obligation" frighten us, and here Adorno can help calm our nerves. In his *Aesthetic Theory* we discover something important about artworks and the way they speak to their

addressee, something we have always known but keep forgetting. Artworks do not speak merely to communicate something. They do not
just tell me a story, sketch a character, show me colors, depict a shape.
They do all of this, of course, but as they do, they ask something of
me. "As they do" makes it sound as though these were two distinct
acts that happen to coincide. A better way of putting it would be: they
tell a story, sketch a character, show me colors, . . . *in a way* that asks
something of me. And what they solicit from me is a certain way of
hearing, a way of hearing attuned to their significance.

Adorno sticks to terms he finds in aesthetics and speaks therefore of
"works of art," but in fact this call is issued by any work that is to have
significance for me—any poetic work. Poetic works have what Adorno
calls a "binding force," and this binding force—a force binding me to
them and them to me—is "essential to works."[22] Cut loose from it, they
drift into ordinariness.

The binding force cannot be isolated in any material feature of a
work, nor in any act of surreptitious meta-communication, whisper-
ing demands into my ear. Andy Warhol's *Brillo Boxes* may look—and
even *be*—identical to the product I find in the shop, yet the two differ
in at least one respect, and it is a profound difference: scouring pads
make no claim on me. They do not ask of me to come to terms with
their significance. True, they issue instructions of what I am to do with
them (instructions I find embedded in their shape and material, in the
history of their use, in what is printed on their packaging), yet they
make no claim. It is the opposite with the *Brillo Boxes*: they arrive with
a claim but no instructions.

A minute ago, I said that poetic works "call on" me and "solicit"
something from me, terms that allow us to imagine the work as an
amicable partner. These terms contrast sharply with Adorno's severe
language of "binding force." Does the poetic work, do art and reflection, forcibly bind me? The word Adorno uses, *Verbindlichkeit*, is more
ambiguous: it names the obliging character of an act, with the full range
of meanings that "oblige" and "obligation" offer: it denotes the coer-
cive force of an oath or contract (as when I am *under* an obligation),
extends to the idea of being in debt (of *having* an obligation), but also
names a sense of gratitude ("I would be obliged . . .") and even an act of
kindness (an obliging gesture, an obliging friend). It tells us that every
invitation, however generous, and every seduction, however alluring,

arrives with a call, and that every call obliges; otherwise, it will have missed its mark.

"Obligation," then, does not do its work by putting a gun to my head, not always, perhaps not even usually. It can be gentle and inviting—obliging in that way. It points to something deeper and more formal than sheer moral duress, namely, that which binds me to something (*obligare*, the dictionary tells me, derives from the Latin verb *ligare*, "to bind"), and this binding force is operative even when the bonds are made of frilly ribbons. Sometimes it is difficult even to make out the bonds exerting their force. I may experience a work as hermetic, utterly scornful of my attention, yet if I am to face it as a work—if it is to be significant to me—I must hear in it a call, the call to take it as the kind of work that asks me—demands of me—to grapple with its significance. It must oblige me.

The "binding force," the obligation issued by a work, is no more than the fact of it addressing me. But also no less. A bond has at least two ends: if a work is to address me, then I must be the sort of being that is capable of feeling addressed, and if I am not, then I must find a way of becoming one. "Art cannot seduce without the complicity of the experiencing subject," Susan Sontag has written.[23] It takes two to tango. If a call is to be heard, I must position myself to hear it. I must—that is where obligation resides: in this *must*—I must give the work the attention for significance that it seeks.

THE AUTHORITY OF THE POETIC

A poetic work demands something of me. Issuing a demand manifests an authority on which it relies, however circumscribed this authority may be, however complicit I may be in its being wielded. But who backs up the authority that *The Trial*, say, has over me? Kafka? Literature? The canon? Where does the "force" in Adorno's "binding force" derive its force?

We know other kinds of bonds: a contract binds people to one another; a deed binds a piece of land to me and me to it; an oath binds me to a god (a state, . . .). These are bonds whose force is licensed by an institution. Is the binding force of a poetic work of this kind? How could it not be, since there is no human life outside institutions?

It is true that my experience of a work cannot help but be molded by institutions (the art and book markets, the gallery, the classroom, and so on), just as it must pass through history, technology, media, and other systems of social organization. But the reverse holds as well: just as it is not wholly conditioned by social markers, it is also not fully in the grip of institutions. Works are too fickle for that. They do both too little and too much: they disappoint by remaining mute when the institution presses them to speak, and then, suddenly, they seize me in ways for which the institution has left me unprepared. Their inconstancy is matched by that of my experience. Even if I was in their grip yesterday, I may not be today. That is why friends of aesthetic education, from Friedrich Schiller on, promise too much when they say that it will deliver humanity to the land of liberty and brotherhood. The undertaking is too volatile to guarantee specific outcomes (except perhaps the outcome of developing resilience amid volatility).

To feel the force running between a work and me, I need both more and less than the assurances an institution offers. More: because I need to feel that the two of us, the work and I, are not merely subjected to a set of practices authorized by an institution, but find ourselves in a common world whose significance is not warranted from above and whose boundaries therefore remain unmapped. Less: because this way of inhabiting the world lacks the order that an institution legislates into being. It is beset by bewilderment and ambivalence.

Which is why intimacy has seemed good to think with: its way of relating to the world is social through and through: no relationship with a person or a thing, not even one that feels wholly private, breaks free from the pull of social systems. The intimate is always more than the private. Yet intimacy also surpasses what social institutions institute. The intimacy between the work and me captures both the thickness of the world we inhabit and its precariousness. Intimacy, when it is there, can feel sturdy as bedrock, yet in a moment it can crack and crumble.

BEING IN HISTORY

Something speaks to me: I use the pronoun in its singular form, because poetic power lies in the singularity of the work. But the singular can also mislead us into imagining that the work and I meet in happy isolation from the rest of the world. A work can speak to me in its singularity only because it appears against a plural background. *The Trial* or *Las Meninas* or *Uncle Tom's Cabin* hardly ever appears out of nowhere, and if it did, it would not mean anything to me. These works come wrapped in layers of cultural significance, which themselves change with time. That is a way of saying that the way a work speaks to me and the way I find to respond (or don't)—that intimacy itself—is not only social but historical.

This is related to the more established idea that the knowledge at stake in the humanities is historical knowledge, which is the gist of hermeneutics. This school of thought teaches that "objects" of historical knowledge are not objects the way atoms or tectonic plates are (or are thought to be), in that they have a temporal dimension the others lack. It is true that the natural sciences aim for knowledge that is not historically conditioned, timeless in that way. But scientists know that their undertaking has a history, that our current insights about matter and life and the cosmos have taken the place of other insights, held to be true with equal fervor, and that other modes of explanation will take the place of what we, today, accept as true. Scientists also know, or could know, that the conception of truth itself has a history, along with its supporting cast of objectivity, proof, experiment, and the rest. In this regard, science is more manifestly historical than are humanistic insights about Homer and Plato.

But that is a history *of* science, not a history *in* science. Yet hermeneutics teaches that being in history is precisely what is true of the humanities: its knowledge does not just *have* a history but *is* historical. How are we to imagine this?

Being in time is not the same thing as being in history, and historicity—being structured by history—is as distinct from temporality as it is from chronology. History requires events to be articulated according to a narrative logic. This logic can take many forms (the theorist Hayden White has provided one typology), but in all its forms it has recourse to the language of motivation, of intention and purpose. To be able to say anything about a historical object—an object *in* history—I must have an idea about the knot of motivations, intentions, and purposes that has brought it about and the knot to which it leads. Which is just what I am called to *avoid* when giving an account of a planet's orbit or a virus's spread. This is where the philosopher Wilhelm

Dilthey sees the chief difference between the historical sciences (the humanities) and the natural sciences: the former, relying on intentions and goals, aim to *understand*, while the latter, bringing to light patterns of material causation, seek to *explain*.

That is one dimension of the historicity of the humanities. There is another, more profound way in which humanistic knowledge is structured historically, and it is this: to be able to understand something in its historical dimension, I must also understand *myself* as a historical being. Historical knowledge is not something to be arrived at from a position of detachment. I am not an observer aloof from what implicates me in the world, but myself a participant in the world. I cannot help but meet things from where I find myself at a given moment, namely, in the here and now.

My encounter with a work and my account of this encounter therefore differs from other such accounts, embedded as they are in situations different from mine. It is for this reason (and not because allegedly "we know more") that criticism and historiography are open-ended enterprises. "Whoever conducts historical studies is always also determined by the fact that he himself experiences history," Hans-Georg Gadamer, an advocate of philosophical hermeneutics, has written. "History is always written anew because the present determines us."[24]

History determines us. The present determines us. We pronounce these words easily, blithely, as though we had pulled them from a fortune cookie, forgetting how heady they are and how frightening. Are all my encounters—with others, with things, with myself—determined by the present, which itself is determined by history? Determined how? When I find that a line from Kafka speaks to me, is that thanks to my history ("my" history?)? And if it fails to touch me, then too? What wiggle room does history leave me in *making* the encounter? I admit to not having answers, which is why these questions shadow the pages of this book, coming into the light only when they can no longer be kept at bay.

BEING IN THE *SAME* HISTORY (TRADITION)

Intimacy in poetic criticism is singular, yet this singularity is impersonal—society courses through it, and so does history. What does that mean? What does this idea allow me to think and say and do, and what does it prevent me from thinking and saying and doing? Gadamer has thought deeply about these questions, so let's stay with him for a moment longer.

The reason the task of historical embedment is important to Gadamer is that it has a direct link to "the business of the historical humanities," whose bottom line, he tells us, is understanding the utterances of the past, or, as he likes to put it, "the fusion of the horizon of the present with the horizon of the past" (55). Without history, no understanding, and without understanding, the humanities are out of business. To succeed, it does not suffice that I place both the "object" of inquiry and myself into history. A further condition must be met: I must understand us as being part of the *same* history. Otherwise, the enterprise of the fusion of horizons runs aground, for you cannot fuse what is completely unlike. The works of the past could speak as loudly as they wished: my ears would remain deaf to their call.

Perhaps that is why monuments from the Maya civilization leave me cold. They are stupendous and they are dazzling. They must have been immensely significant to the people who built and used them, even to those who dreaded them; to them especially. I squint at them in the glare of the bright day and dare not confess to myself that I am at a loss. I have no idea what they want of me. Then, like everyone else, I pull out my phone and take pictures. These complicated edifices leave me perplexed, yet it is an untroubled perplexity, one that swiftly yields to curiosity and soothes itself with information—the perplexity of a tourist. Gadamer would say that I fail to understand because I fail to share a history, enough of a history, with the world in which these structures are meaningful. It is an incomprehension born of thin intimacy.

But—and Gadamer does not say this often enough—that does not mean that thick intimacy, nurtured by my sense that my history links me to the work speaking to me, allows me to hear it the way it wishes to be heard. Sharing a history does not always put me on the path of understanding. Being in the same history does not make us, the work and me, into allies who move in lockstep. We are more like friends; we are intimate strangers.

Intimacy, while enabling comprehension, also sharpens the edge of incomprehension. It changes the texture of non-understanding, perhaps more drastically even than that of understanding. Now I fail to

understand not because I fail to know the code or because I have committed an error in the arithmetic of decipherment but because another
way of being has left me dumbfounded. How different the incomprehension born of thick intimacy is when compared to the bafflement
I feel before the Maya structures: because I face the strangeness of
something I know from inside—a parable from the Bible or a shadow
in a painting I love—it finds a way of getting under my skin.

Gadamer has been much criticized, and rightly, for positing understanding as the grail of historical work; no need adding to the com-
plaints. Scholars and critics have pushed back against a tendency they
see in hermeneutics to smooth things out, and so they dwell on wrinkles and folds in the text. In Gadamer's defense it must be admitted
that the thought that incomprehension is a constant hazard bedeviling
comprehension is not truly new; it merely calls attention to the fact
that comprehension is always at risk of misadventure. But who said
this business was risk-free?

In any case, the important point is not to take sides in the skirmish
between understanding and its foes but to find out what a work allows
me—what it urges me—to say and to do. Understanding is in play,
and therefore of interest, to the exact degree that it prompts me to
make something of my present moment. What and how I understand
depends on what and how I end up making.

Let us grant that a work becomes significant to me only when I take
it to be involved in the same history in which I find myself. But what
does sameness entail here? What qualifies as being part of the same
history and what not?

Suppose I attend a flamenco performance: by the lights of hermeneutic theory, I remain insensible to it if I do not find myself in an
unbroken chain of historical causes and effects linking me to the event.
But under which conditions do I come to stand at the end of a chain
that, somewhere down the line, has flamenco as one of its links? Only
if I have lived my life under the Andalusian sun? What if I moved there
from a pale and gloomy place? What if I am a devotee of flamenco—
study it, sing it, and dance it passionately—but in Indiana? Or in India?
Does it *really* speak to me then, or do I merely imagine that? Millions
of people on this globe are moved to sincere tears of sorrow by the diary of Anne Frank—is it because they share a history with that work?

Gadamer seeks to solve the riddle of historical continuity with the
notion of tradition: it is, he thinks, what issues the warrant for being

spoken to by the past. He writes: "Our usual relationship to the past is not characterized by distancing and freeing ourselves from tradition. Rather, we are always situated within traditions, and this is no objectifying process—i.e., we do not conceive of what tradition says as something other, something alien. It is always part of us." Because it is always part of us, "the anticipation of meaning that governs our understanding of a text is not an act of subjectivity, but proceeds from the commonality that binds us to the tradition."[25] Tradition is not something I choose; I am part of it and it part of me. It is not something alien but is woven into my being. It governs what becomes significant to me.

Has tradition made the question of historical filiation and, further downstream, the phenomenon of intimacy less mysterious? Difficult to say. I find the paintings in the caves of Lascaux and Chauvet unutterably powerful. Is it that they and I are part of a tradition? Which tradition would that be? Hardly "the tradition of European painting." Well, what then? The tradition of using color? The tradition of making significant marks? The tradition of loving beautiful things? If these are traditions, then there would not seem to exist a human act to which I am not bound by some tradition. Besides, if tradition is to be credited—or blamed—for what binds me to the cave paintings, how is it that a bond to something so impossibly remote has escaped damage (through forgetting, neglect, or violence) while the Maya monuments, not to mention countless other works far closer in space and in time, have slipped away, if ever they did belong to "my" tradition?

The worry is that "tradition" may be so rubbery a substance as to lose all coherence as a concept. One moment it is elastic enough to bind me to Paleolithic life; the next, its rigidity keeps me from gaining purchase on things close at hand. Not to mention that a musty and conservative air clings to it. Would scrapping it help? To be replaced by what? How to give texture to the intimate bond that, mysteriously, establishes itself between a work and me? And how to describe that texture to account for the fact, equally mysterious, that sometimes a bond is *prevented* from forming?

A BASTARD OF HISTORY

What hides in plain view of the concept of tradition—also of its substitutes: history, culture, identity—is a conundrum that is at bottom not philosophical but political: these concepts adjudicate who, and under which provisos, is entitled to have certain kinds of experience and who is not. They decide—they exist to decide—who and what makes part of a tradition—a history, a culture, an identity—and who and what does not. If for reasons of tradition—or of history, culture, or identity—I am judged to have no business with Kafka's writings, or with the horses galloping away on the walls of the Chauvet cave, or the pyramid at Uxmal, then I am out of luck. Whatever counterclaim I make will be brushed off as illegitimate or immoral or delusional, unless—and that is a big unless—I manage to bring about a shift in the concept of tradition (of history, culture, identity) in a way that legitimates and therefore accommodates my move.

What is at stake, then, in the politics of hearing and of speaking, which is also the politics of intimacy, is not whether my claim to having been spoken to (having heard) and to speaking is granted or refused but, rather, how to shape the adjudicating conception—whatever its title—so as to grant or to refuse the claim.

Look, for instance, at how James Baldwin, while on a walk in a remote Swiss village in the early 1950s, considers the inhabitants (and, if you have the inclination, try to map the exact trajectories of history, tradition, culture, and identity as they collide here):

> These people cannot be, from the point of view of power, strangers anywhere in the world; they have made the modern world, in effect, even if they do not know it. The most illiterate among them is related, in a way that I am not, to Dante, Shakespeare, Michelangelo, Aeschylus, Da Vinci, Rembrandt, and Racine; the cathedral at Chartres says something to them which it cannot say to me, as indeed would New York's Empire State Building, should anyone here ever see it. Out of their hymns and dances come Beethoven and Bach. Go back a few centuries and they are in their full glory—but I am in Africa, watching the conquerors arrive.[26]

So ferocious is the passage's intelligence, so vigorous the blow to the skull that it delivers, that it takes time—it took me some years—to collect one's wits and ask: really? Is it really the case that the most illiterate of the Swiss is related to Dante and Shakespeare in a way Baldwin is not?

And the answer must be: yes, it *is* the case, provided—and now the fine print—provided you understand "being related to" the way Baldwin does, namely, as flowing from the blood of kinship, and provided you understand history as does Baldwin: nothing but a curse whose judgment must be suffered. Baldwin tends to a tragic view of history more commonly encountered among European writers. "Joyce is right about history being a nightmare," he notes, "but it may be the nightmare from which no one can awaken. People are trapped in history and history is trapped in them" (166–67). I use "tragic" in its original sense, for this conception of history rests directly, not on Aeschylus, but on Sophocles, as Baldwin explains in an essay on Richard Wright's novel *Native Son*:

> It is a sentimental error, therefore, to believe that the past is dead; it means nothing to say that it is all forgotten, that the Negro himself has forgotten it. It is not a question of memory. Oedipus did not remember the thongs that bound his feet; nevertheless the marks they left testified to that doom toward which his feet were leading him. The man does not remember the hand that struck him, the darkness that frightened him, as a child; nevertheless, the hand and the darkness remain with him, indivisible from himself forever.[27]

The violence of history—the violence that *is* history—remains, and it remains *forever*. History is a nightmare from which no one—*no one*—can awaken. People are trapped in history and history is trapped in them. Baldwin is still in Africa, while the Swiss villagers, kinsmen of the "*Herrenvolk*" (169), stand to receive as their patrimony the cathedral of Chartres. That is what Baldwin is saying.

It is this unforgiving idea of history—of culture, of inheritance, of tradition (tradition, he writes, expresses "nothing more than the long and painful experience of a people" [36])—it is this tragic mood that attracted me to the essay and that also frightened me, and frightens me still. I desperately want it not to be true. What I have made of my life, and therefore also this book, is predicated on the essay *not* telling the truth, not the whole truth anyway. Otherwise, my experience of Kafka speaking to me, of Kleist and Barthes and Baldwin speaking to me, would be nothing but delusion. What I have written about the intimacy in being spoken to and the urgency of speaking would be wishful thinking, if it could be called thinking, and I a dupe, an impostor.

The truth is that my biography has not placed me squarely among the *Herrenvolk*, and so I come to the works that have sustained me and also vexed me all my life—to this tradition (let's call it that)—from the

side, and my access has remained oblique. It was strange to be reading Schiller and Sophocles and Ionesco's *Bald Soprano* in Tehran: you
needed a stretchable imagination to believe these works were meant
for us, my classmates and me. Yet it was also exhilarating, because it
expressed the idea that people are *not* forever trapped in history, at least
not in a *single* history. It presented the possibility that even when works
are not obviously addressed to me, I can still find ways of hearing them
speak to me. I need not forever remain deaf to them, not even to the
Maya monuments. Fallacies all and lies?

Baldwin's essay is not about the Swiss villagers, who are no more
than extras in this production, but about himself, the "Stranger in the
Village," and the village that matters to him lies not in Switzerland but
in America; it is America. Like much of his writings, this essay is about
being a stranger in America. His estrangement stems from the savage
dispossession of the past exacted not only on those Africans shipped
to America but also on their descendants, including those who centuries later find themselves strolling in the Alps. But as Baldwin does
not tire of repeating, this is an estrangement not *from* America, but an
estrangement *in* America. The stranger makes America, and America,
in turn, makes the stranger.

This is the point where the essay opens a door to me. Not that har-
mony has suddenly been established and horizons have been fused;
not that I now feel Baldwin's pain; not that suffering has been revealed
to be a universal condition of humanity. Rather, I am able to see in
Baldwin's, and in America's, strangeness some of the strangeness that
prevails between the "tradition" and myself, and since tradition is si-
lently part of me, that means, in effect, that I am able to see and to feel
some of the strangeness in myself. Baldwin's words resonate most with
me not when they dislodge him from the West and place him in Africa,
but when they acknowledge him to be a "bastard of the West." Now
I see that his history and his passions, so evidently running athwart
tradition, renew and remake tradition. Here is the passage from an
autobiographical essay in which he seeks to sort out the question of
birth and birthright:

> The most crucial time in my own development came when I was forced
> to recognize that I was a kind of bastard of the West; when I followed
> the line of my past I did not find myself in Europe but in Africa. And

this meant that in some subtle way, in a really profound way, I brought to Shakespeare, Bach, Rembrandt, to the stones of Paris, to the cathedral at Chartres, and to the Empire State Building, a special attitude. These were not really my creations, they did not contain my history; I might search in them in vain forever for any reflection of myself. I was an interloper; this was not my heritage. At the same time I had no other heritage which I could possibly hope to use—I had certainly been unfitted for the jungle or the tribe. I would have to appropriate these white centuries, I would have to make them mine—I would have to accept my special attitude, my special place in this scheme—otherwise I would have no place in any scheme.[28]

The recognition—a "forced" recognition, he admits—that he must "appropriate these white centuries," must take possession of what he knows not to be his creations, goes hand in hand with another recognition, likely also forced, the he, like "the American Negro," "is not a visitor to the West, but a citizen there, an American; as American as the Americans who despise him, the Americans who fear him, the Americans who love him" (177).

These two recognitions, linked claims to appropriation—one cultural, the other political—lead, thirty years on, to a reflection on the power of history that leaves behind the mythic idea of history as tragic inevitability and cracks open a space that will accommodate the act of making for oneself a "special place in this scheme." It is 1984 when Baldwin, now sixty, writes: "I am what time, circumstance, history, have made of me, certainly, but I am, also, much more than that. So are we all."[29] Yes, all of us are made by history, by tradition, by culture, by identity, but we are not made by these entirely; there is "much more than that."

You do not need to read Baldwin to know (though when you read him, it is hard to forget) that all of us are not composed of the same ratio of history and what is "much more" than history. All of us are bastards of history but some more so than others: some bastards inherit a greater share of the patrimony, while others, dispossessed, find themselves urged to make more of this patrimony, *much* more. Appropriation can take the form of plunder, but it can also name poetic making and remaking.

Now I see that the idea of surpassing the history in which one finds oneself trapped is more than merely adumbrated in "Stranger in the Village," yet in my panic I chose to overlook it. Baldwin writes that the Swiss villagers are related to Dante, Shakespeare, Michelangelo, and the rest "in a way that I am not," which I now take to mean that he, too, is related to this tradition, but differently. The same goes for the cathedral in Chartres: though it "says something to [the villagers] which it cannot say to me," it does not remain mute when facing Baldwin, but speaks to him in a different tongue. He says as much in the essay's final pages:

> The cathedral at Chartres, I have said, says something to the people of this village which it cannot say to me; but it is important to understand that this cathedral says something to me which it cannot say to them. (177)

And what might the cathedral say to him that it cannot say to them?

> Perhaps they are struck by the power of the spires, the glory of the windows; but they have known God, after all, longer than I have known him, and in a different way, and I am terrified by the slippery bottomless well to be found in the crypt, down which heretics were hurled to death, and by the obscene, inescapable gargoyles jutting out of the stone and seeming to say that God and the devil can never be divorced. I doubt that the villagers think of the devil when they face a cathedral because they have never been identified with the devil. But I must accept the status which myth, if nothing else, gives me in the West before I can hope to change the myth. (177–78)

The intimacy I can have with something—with a cathedral, with any work—takes its form from the history that has made me and in which I find myself, the history that is my present moment. That provides me with resources, and with limits, that differ from those at the disposal of others, saddled as they are with their own histories. But, like everyone else, I do not know my present moment, cannot comprehend my resources and my limits, not fully enough to give an accounting of my ways of hearing and my ways of making. They escape and exceed me. Which is why I can hear and make in ways that surpass and remake my history.

PART 2

I Must Tell You About It

(URGENCY)

Once more, our three-step:

> Something speaks to me.
> I must tell you about it.
> But I don't know how.

You recall the scene: holding Kafka's *Trial*, I read aloud to the students a passage and discovered with a start that I had nothing to say about it. I read it again. Nothing. Getting nervous, I skipped to another passage, then another. It was now clear, to the students and finally also to me, that I was not up to these lines of Kafka's. I lacked the words to say something about them, something *real*, something other than the platitudes I had passed off in the past.

When I realized that day that instead of offering the students analysis and interpretation, all I could manage was to repeat the same mute gesture ("Look! Listen!"), I gave up what remained of my plan and confessed that all I wanted to do—all I felt I could do—was to "let the text speak for itself," which was a fancy way of saying that I wished I could read aloud passage after passage, even the whole novel, had there been time. This move, born of desperation rather than of foresight, changed everything in the dynamic of the class: the blockage dissolved, and the discussion flowed.

Not that the key to *The Trial* had miraculously fallen into our laps. Understanding remained out of reach. What had changed was that now possessing it seemed less pressing. The way had opened for us, the students and me, to ask instead what urges us toward interpretation— toward any sort of response. Why does it feel insufficient simply to read Kafka's lines and say not another word?

UNDERSTANDING AND MAKING

How to understand, how to describe the urgency of responding to something I face, an urgency that can take the form of an impotent muteness, of stuttering, of hemming and hawing? Zoom out from Kafka to see the basic structure: Something speaks to me, and because "I want someone to catch my overflow of pleasure" or of perplexity, I feel I must tell you.[1] Something calls; I respond. Call followed by response.

But followed how? How is response linked to call? Does it follow like thunder follows lightning (same phenomenon, different guise)? Does it echo the call (a diminution)? Is it the explosion that follows after a fuse has been lit (an augmentation)? It could take any of these forms, yet none grasps the logic. My response, while prompted— invited, incited—by the call, is not caused by it. The urgency I feel is of a different order. It emerges from that "binding force" that Theodor Adorno discovers between a poetic work and me, a force not to be found by physics, but no less potent than the laws of nature.

How then to imagine the articulation of the two, of call and response? One way of imagining it would be to take literally the idea of "something speaking to me" and my then "responding." Hans-Georg Gadamer does that; he thinks of call and response as a conversation between two people. Gadamer is a philosopher and an authority on classical Greek thinking, and so, for him, the essence of conversation lies in a dialogue in which interlocutors set out to know the truth. By his lights, every conversation, even when it does not have the search for knowledge as its theme, "necessarily has the structure of question and answer."[2] Call and response, then, is nothing but question and answer.

Does that seem right? Is it right to say that at the heart of every conversation lies a Platonic dialogue, and that when a work speaks to me and I feel pressed to respond, I am unwittingly engaged in a philosophical quest? When speaking about a poetic work, must we, as Gadamer insists, "discover the question which it answers" (364)? The logic of question and answer makes sense if, like Gadamer, you posit *understanding* as the object—the purpose and aim—of the response to a work.

But poetic criticism has a different orientation. Its aim is, to cite Friedrich Schlegel again, to "replenish the work, rejuvenate it, shape it afresh."[3] The way the poetic critic responds to the work is, then, a way of *doing*, of saying or making something new that is prompted by something old. Poetic criticism seeks to understand what it encounters to the extent that it *makes* something, and the something it makes is *sense*. It makes sense.

That is not how things are described mostly. Mostly, understanding and making are seen as distinct, even polar, activities, and once a split has opened between gathering old sense and manufacturing new sense, it is hard to close. Now the two sides stiffen. They become types, characters in an allegorical drama—Interpretation versus Creation; Hermeneutics versus Poetics; Secondary versus Primary Literature. In the last decades, critics have more and more turned interpretation into a bookish, monkish practice, which leads them to covet its meaty opposite number, whatever shape it takes on a given day: Embodiment, Affect, the Ecstatic, and the rest. Susan Sontag's essay "Against Interpretation" is a good place to look. Interpretation, she finds, is for philistines, and since she is definitely not a philistine, she can declare: "In place of a hermeneutics we need an erotics of art." Who can be against that?

It is true that interpretation and its antagonists are ideal types, and true also that everyone knows it. But everyone also forgets: you play with these figures long enough, and the ideal starts becoming real. Take "presence," introduced by the scholar Hans Ulrich Gumbrecht. His presence is everything interpretation is not: it "exclusively appeal[s] to the senses," "reestablish[es] our contact with the things of the world outside the subject/object paradigm," has as its "dominant self-reference . . . the body," and so on.[4]

What have we learned? That it is possible to manhandle interpretation *and* presence. For when I come face to face with things that hold significance for me, I am not *either* struck dumb by a bolt of ecstatic truth that is blissfully devoid of meaning (what kind of truth would that be?) *or* on the scholar's treadmill, chasing a morsel of meaning just out of reach while feeling nothing. When epiphanies do occur, they flicker with shards of meaning. And even the most labored scholarly excavation has woven into it a passion for things. Interpretation and presence do not reside on opposite "poles" or in distinct "layers" between which one is to "oscillate," as Gumbrecht recommends (xv; 107), but pervade experience.

One trouble with cartoonish dramas is that they give the villain too little credit: if interpretation dwells in a zone so utterly segregated from joy, from flesh, from life, you have to wonder why or even how anyone goes near it. But the other, more serious trouble is that the villain gets too much credit: once interpretation gets going, everything turns into meaning. It is true that when we stop thinking of interpretation as a technique of decoding occult messages and understand it instead as the way my ear is tuned to the world, we see how vast it is. Maurice Merleau-Ponty, the poet-phenomenologist, is right to insist that meaning does not constitute a special region cordoned off from the rest of the world. "There is not a human word, not a gesture, even one which is the outcome of habit or absent-mindedness, which has not some meaning," he writes.[5]

Meaning is everywhere, yes, but meaning is also fragile. Once encountered, it is not a quantum we can gather and pile on other bits of meaning, but something that may slip away into meaninglessness at any time. Who has not been in a fluid conversation that abruptly loses its rhythm because I think I have detected a quiver of the lip in my interlocutor, a quiver that *could* mean something but then again might not? The opposite happens too: a word at the tip of my tongue is released through a gesture someone else makes, and again I cannot make out if that gesture was meant to be meaningful. (That is the subject of Heinrich von Kleist's marvelous essay "On the Gradual Production of Thoughts While Speaking," written right around 1805.)

If the account of our experience with meaning—if criticism—is to become richer and truer, then we must acknowledge what we know already, namely, that meaning gained in interpretation is always at a risk of loss. It is at stake. It is in play. What *is* present in every encounter is significance, which is not this or that meaning, but meaning-at-stake, meaning-in-play. We critics like to fret about the range of meaning (polysemy, ambiguity, and so on) and the way it is prone to mutate without warning (it is "slippery," we say), but for all its show of daring, that game is played well *within* the touchlines of meaning.

The more disquieting, and more significant, play is right on the line between meaning and its lack. Why more significant? Because there can be no meaning without the risk of it crossing into meaninglessness at *any* moment, and so *every* meaning cannot help but play right along the line. Clifford Geertz, the poet-anthropologist, spins it out for us:

was that a wink I saw on your face, or was it a twitch, and if a twitch: was it a nervous twitch that betrays a bad conscience (say), was it a pretend-twitch trying to fool me, or was it *just* a twitch?[6] (Have a look at the climax of Hitchcock's *The Young and Innocent* to see how deliciously one can stage a twitch perched right on the cliff edge of meaning.)

I've gotten off my path. What do winks and twitches have to do with poetic criticism, with the way it makes sense? The point—one point—is that, because sense is not a durable good you can keep in storage, gathering old sense always involves making new sense. There is no primary literature that does not come after—in response to, provoked by—some yet more primary thing. There is no interpretation that is not also creation, and no hermeneutics wholly bereft of erotics.

In poetic criticism, ways of understanding and ways of making are not opposed. I understand so that I can make, and through making my understanding changes. The two participate in one another. Indeed, participation is the way poetic criticism manifests itself: as I speak about *The Trial*, as I stutter my way into it, I take part in *The Trial*. I make sense of it and, making sense, make it part of my life.

MAKING THE NEW BY REMAKING THE OLD

Poetic criticism makes something new. But what kind of thing is this, and what kind of making? If poetic criticism is not retrospective in orientation (as Gadamer imagines it), then some writers conclude that its mode of making must be prospective, even prophetic. Emerson is among these. "The eyes of man are set in his forehead, not in his hindhead," he notes. That being the case, he counsels the scholar to cast off books and other ballast of the past to free the mind for the one pursuit that matters: "the act of creation—the act of thought."[7] Rather than getting bogged down deciphering someone else's meaning, the scholar—the poet, the orator, Thinking Man (Emerson uses many names)—must make new meaning. The watchword is plain: "We hear, that we may speak" (60). Were Emerson addressing not the Harvard class of 1837 but us, today, he would note how distant we scholars, we critics and interpreters, remain from making his maxim our own: so anxious are we to record every last syllable echoing in our archives that we forget to speak.

It is a powerful line of thinking—maybe too powerful. Reading Emerson, you find yourself strong-armed into taking sides between options that, upon reflection, turn out to be more entangled than he allows and that, in fact, derive their power from being implicated in one another: you feel you must choose between the act of interpretation and that of creation, between what lies behind and what waits ahead, between hearing and speaking—as though the gain of the one were the loss of the other. But is it? Does creative speaking not entail creative hearing? "One must be an inventor to read well," Emerson declares at one point (60). Agreed, but the fact that the proposition holds even when flipped means that reading well and inventing well are so tightly coiled that pulling them apart is a fool's errand. Who can decide whether *Paradise Lost* is an Emersonian act of creation, its eyes fixed forward and indifferent to all that faces its hindhead, or a turn to the past to grapple with the significance of a book—of *the* Book? We know it is both—emphatically both. In making something new, poetic criticism remakes something found.

In response to the question of what form poetic criticism takes, of what kind of making it entails, should I then hold up *Paradise Lost*? After all, the poem is an exemplary instance of the urgency in hearing that is also an urgency of speaking. Yet I waver; second thoughts rear their heads. Can one really call the poem "criticism"? Would that not offend the poem *and* criticism? If *Paradise Lost* is an instance of criticism, what then isn't? And so on. These qualms no doubt reveal how set in my ways I am; surely they would melt away if I just learned to see criticism more capaciously.

Others have done that. When Friedrich Schlegel coins the term "poetic criticism" (actually, *poetische Kritik*), he has in mind a form of making that will—I quoted it a few pages ago—"replenish the work, rejuvenate it, shape it afresh."[8] Here, *Hamlet* is the work being replenished, rejuvenated, reshaped, and *Wilhelm Meister's Apprenticeship* the work doing the replenishing, rejuvenating, reshaping—the work of poetic criticism. Is it less strange to think of Goethe's novel as a criticism of *Hamlet* than of Milton's epic as a criticism of the book of Genesis? Probably: we take for granted that, starting with Romanticism, the gesture of reflexivity—the *re-* in replenish, rejuvenate, reshape—characterizes literature and other arts in ways that do not hold for older works.

That may be true, or it may just have the ring of truth. Scholars of earlier periods keep pointing out that works going back deep into antiquity stand in no less layered and complex a relationship to their forerunners—are no less critical—than later works. We can credit this claim without forsaking the idea of historical change. For some purposes, it makes sense to identify a pattern or "zeitgeist" (or however one names the collection of features that are said to characterize a "period" or "age"), yet that would hardly tell us anything worth knowing about the ways a work, singular as it is, may be an instance of poetic criticism.

Poetic criticism is an idea that Charles Baudelaire, too, endorses. In an essay called "What Good Is Criticism?," which also gets at the question of what good criticism is, he declares that "the best criticism is the kind that is amusing and poetic" and that "the best review of a painting could be a sonnet or an elegy."[9] This might lead us to think that poetry can be found only in what is commonly called "poetry," a catchall for lyric genres. Yet the poetic has nothing to do with the classification of books nor with the way lines break on a page. Rather, it is a way of intensifying the world by making something new while remaking something found. Poetry can be made and therefore found anywhere, not just on the poetry shelf of the bookstore. The flip side is that there is no telling if it can be found even there: nothing ensures that sonnets or elegies will hold a higher concentration of poetry than a piece of criticism or a piece of plastic.

The way to read Baudelaire's quip is not as hemming in the poetic into a few known genres but as stretching criticism, not just its form but its very matter. To do that, criticism must be revealed as a stretchable substance capable of assuming new shapes. The best criticism *is* plastic. When I put down the book that speaks to me to tell you about it, nothing predicts what this telling might look like. It can take the form of an epic poem or of a sonnet. It can appear in a gesture or a picture or a movie. Sometimes—on some days and in the company of some people—it breaks out as a stutter or as panicked muteness: I hear, and I find myself tongue-tied. Often, though, it takes the form of an essay, a canonical essay like those by Emerson or Adorno, or an essay in atypical guise: a fragment by Schlegel, a paragraph by Nietzsche, a chapter by Eve Sedgwick, a book by Roland Barthes.

Yet, no matter its form, if this telling is to convey the urgency to share the experience that someone has had with a book or other significant thing (which really means: to *make* that experience in shar-

ing it), it cannot be a detached or isolated act. It cannot become un-
hinged from what came before but must somehow remain hinged to
the encounter—with the vagueness of "somehow" bearing witness to
the endless variability of the telling. We hear that we may speak, and
in speaking—in orating and singing, in mumbling and stuttering—we
acknowledge that we have heard.

LEARNING NOT TO CONCLUDE

When I say that the work speaks to me and prompts me to act, I acknowledge the fact that it is, first of all, not I who have something to say
about it but, on the contrary, that it says something about me, something I did not know how to say myself. It reveals something about
me that, again, is not a piece of theoretical self-knowledge (it doesn't
"hold up a mirror"), but a way of making I did not know I had in me.

What kind of making is this? What shape does it take? Some pages
ago I said that Roland Barthes's *Empire of Signs* prompts me to develop
an intimacy with the accent of his voice. I also said that his essay is not
reducible to a set of linked concepts—a thesis—but exceeds the grasp
of concepts with the vibrancy of its language. That makes it sound as
though the text asks my complicity in holding up the "poetic" against
the "conceptual." Once we go down that road, we picture the "poetic"
in poetic criticism as a way of siding with everything meaty that poetry
is thought to deliver—sensation, passion, vivacity—against the bone-
dry ideas of philosophy and scholarship, which stack up to make a "co-
lumbarium of concepts" (as Nietzsche calls it).[10] Before long we would,
like Susan Sontag, pit the "sensual capability" aroused by art against
the "hypertrophy of the intellect" so as to denounce all the more vigor-
ously "interpretation [as] the revenge of the intellect upon art."[11]

But that would misapprehend Barthes's writing and what it urges
me to do, and hence misapprehend poetic criticism. Barthes does not, I
think, pit the poetic (or artistic) against the conceptual (or philosophical). Just the opposite: his essay eagerly taps into the powers of the
intellect. *Empire of Signs* fuses poetic and philosophical elements so
promiscuously that it would be a fool's errand to divide them so they
may be tallied, one against the other. It is too busy experimenting with
ideas to bother deconstructing them.

What, then, do I do? Nothing can stop me from falling into old habits and taking up deconstruction or critique or polemics, least of all the work I hold before me. Yet I waver, not for any warning it may have issued, but because the mood in its pages takes me elsewhere. Barthes's essay, I notice, is not dogmatic enough to devote itself to exposing the pretensions of philosophy or to deplore the betrayal of art by interpretation, nor do I find anywhere in its pages the opposite conclusion, that the poetic and the conceptual are one and the same.

In fact, I find no conclusion.

The text does not conclude, and neither does the book: it simply ends in midparagraph, abruptly and arbitrarily, forgoing any tonal quiver that might announce the finale expected of a monograph. This way of ending says: the book could just as well have ended elsewhere, at some earlier point. It also says: it could end later, in parts unwritten, parts left to readers to imagine and perhaps to write.

Though we know they exist, it is always startling to come upon such books, for they testify to writers who remain untroubled, pleased even, by the fact that their words are to be superseded by other words. Which writer is generous enough to give readers not only words, but also the freedom *not* to read them? In our case, we realize that we need not have waited for the last page to recognize what sort of a book this is. Once alerted, you see that it lets us know on every page. Look once more at our sashimi passage:

> . . . the edible substance is without a precious heart, without a buried power, without a vital secret: no Japanese dish is endowed with a *center* . . . ; here everything is the ornament of another ornament: . . . food is never anything but a collection of fragments, none of which appears privileged by an order of ingestion; to eat is not to respect a menu (an itinerary of dishes), but to select, with a light touch of the chopsticks, sometimes one color, sometimes another . . .

Is it a stretch to say that the Japanese meal gives Barthes the structure he needs to write about this very meal? Change a few words, and you have an abstract of the book:

> The book's poetic substance is without a precious heart, without a buried power, without a vital secret: nowhere is its exposition endowed with a *center* . . . ; here everything is the ornament of another orna-

> ment: the reflections on the meaning of food are never anything but a collection of fragments, none of which appears privileged by an order of presentation; to read is not to respect an outline (an itinerary of chapters), but to select sometimes one passage, sometimes another . . .

A key theme of the book is that "Japan" is an empire without a center. ("Japan," the place he writes about, Barthes insists, is not the same as Japan, though the two bear a striking resemblance.) In this empire, there is no sign weighty enough to pin down the other signs. This insight manifests itself on the grand scale of the country's political geography, in which the central location in the central city, the emperor's palace in Tokyo, stands drained of power, as it does on the domestic scale of dinner tables, where, absent a cut of meat, the meal is not arranged around the flesh of a sacrificial beast that lends meaning to everything else.

Now we see that this truth about the empire of signs extends to *Empire of Signs* itself. Not endowed with a center, the book could have opened and closed elsewhere and otherwise. And—this is pivotal for what I, the reader, am to *do*—it can be extended along every dimension, yielding countless *Empires of Signs*, each different from the one I hold, yet all coming into being in response to it. The preface, where readers seek the stage directions to the scene of reading, announces that "text and image, interlacing, seek to ensure the circulation and exchange" of signifiers (xi). Circulation and exchange, not the conclusion of signifiers: that is how *Empire of Signs* urges its reader to breach its printed boundaries in directions unimagined by its author. The book keeps going in other books. It prompts me to ask not—not mainly— "what does it mean?" but rather "what do I do next?"

Have we not rediscovered Friedrich Schlegel's notion of poetic criticism, which we came across a few pages ago? "Poetic criticism," he writes nearly two hundred years before Barthes, "does not . . . merely say what the thing is, and where it stands and should stand in the world." Rather than determining the work's essence and position, the poetic critic "will want to present anew what has been presented, and form once more what has already been formed."[12]

It is true that nothing inherent to the work gives unambiguous preference to poetic criticism. Nothing prevents other forms of critique from moving in and doing their thing. Their results are by no means wrong; on the contrary: they are too right and too powerful. With a few shrewd moves, they checkmate us naïve readers. We throw up our hands in defeat, but we cannot help feeling a little cheated—cheated, not because rules were breached, but because the game has abruptly come to an end.

Barthes's writing, too, can be subjected to such procedures. What is to stop me? Yet if I allow myself to listen to it, I might hear in it a call to suspend the question of where the poetic stops and the philosophical begins, not because it is illegitimate or impossible to pose, but because suspending it opens another door to the work. I permit myself to learn to hum its melody without knowing all the words. Before long, I can shift from a major to a minor key, or vice versa, or go off key. That works for as long as I keep myself from prying apart tune and argument, though I know there to be a difference. The moment I tally the differences between the *how* and the *what* and begin subtracting the one from the other in the hope of ending up with a clean set of propositions, the losses pile up, until the work itself is spent, save for a few assertions that I could have picked up anywhere.

When I give in to the work's solicitation, I allow Barthes's book to continue in other books—in this one, for example. And not in books alone: any product or behavior will do that becomes the vehicle for continuing where Barthes has left off: a film, a song, a conversation, even—why not—a meal.

More likely than not, somewhere in the origin story of our passage there is a meal at which Roland Barthes plucks pieces of sushi from a platter, puts them in his mouth, chews, swallows, and ingests them. The food then undergoes a double transformation: as the fish becomes the flesh of Barthes's body, the meal is transmuted into a memory or a dream, which somehow leads to the writing of strings of words, which themselves undergo changes before being fixed in print. (I am fabulating, for who can know where writing finds its origin.) That could be the end of it, but it is not, for now something marvelous happens: the book finds its way into my hands and some passages in it produce in me an intense craving for Japanese food. In a process of reverse-transmutation, Barthes's words become my lunch, over which I may even talk about *Empire of Signs* to a friend, which in turn could lead to writing the words you are reading.

A phrase in one of Walter Benjamin's notebooks, which always seemed mysterious, now gains some weight and specificity. Benjamin writes:

> In the case of great works, art is merely a transitional stage. They were something else (in the course of their gestation) and become something else again (in the state of criticism).[13]

Here, then, is one thing that Barthes's words urge me to do: to eat them—to ingest them, ruminate on them, digest them, use them as an aphrodisiac, and make more of them.

TACT

I want to say: poetic criticism entails eating the words someone has served up and metabolizing them into new things; words, for example. But I also want to say that poetic criticism demands tact, and tact is something that we who study, who write about and instruct others on poetic works mostly lack. We arrive with gear. We find things "problematic." It does not embarrass us—on the contrary—that our ideas are ungainly and our tone entitled.

Yet tact is what you need if you are to do what Barthes's writing wants you to do: to learn its rhythm and pick up where it leaves off. If you know German, you may know that already: *Takt* means both "tact" and "beat, rhythm, measure." (Apparently, English has this meaning too, though the *OED*'s most recent usage example for the musical meaning dates from 1891.) To have *Taktgefühl* is to have a sense of tact or a sense of rhythm (or both). You need tact to learn tapping, and as you tap, you hone your tact. The two—learning to tap and learning tact—go together, one feeding and fortifying the other.

To develop an ear for Barthes's words, I need tact. I need it not because it adds one more arrow to my quiver, one more method or "theoretical approach" with which to puncture the text's subterfuges and pin down its shifty designs, but because it prompts me to disarm. Tact has something stuffy about it, a courtliness that seems to belong to another time, but it is much deeper than mere etiquette. It is an ethos, an ethical practice. It is a way of giving care, and this way of caring takes the form of restraint: I omit doing something that, by rights, I am entitled to do.

Omitting actions for moral reasons is itself common enough. In fact, the basic vector of morality seems to point to prohibition, which is why commandments harp on what thou shalt *not* do. But tact is strange: it too urges avoidance, yet it steers me away, not from wickedness, but from the truth. Not that I forget the truth; I know it, and still I pass over it in silence, or at least handle it with care. I am about to say, "I told you so"—because I *did*, in fact, tell you so—but bite my tongue to spare you the sting of shame. You see on my arm the big, dark stain that is a birthmark, and I see you see it, but you say nothing, which leaves me grateful. Tact is the tacit acknowledgment that the truth is a complicated possession: sometimes it heals a breach in the world, and sometimes it can be wielded like a blade. Tact is a way of staying my hand to keep you from being lacerated by the truth.

How does this relate to hearing Barthes, and how to the urge to speak when I have heard? If we think of tact as caring just for another person or entity, then its relevance here remains obscure. But tact reaches beyond the other. When I am tactful, I care not merely for someone else (for a person or a group, say), but also for the social world in which this other and I are embedded. That is why tact is not just a feeling but, in the words of Hans-Georg Gadamer, "a mode of knowing and a mode of being."[14] I can always call out the other in the name of a truth—whatever truth: moral, aesthetic, scientific, legal, social—and this may even add to my stock of righteous power, but I risk sabotaging the dealings that are just then under way. These dealings may be as local and particular as the conversation you and I are having, or may encompass the entire social structure: one tactless gesture, and the whole thing caves in. Witness what can happen when a little girl broadcasts that the emperor has no clothes, something everyone knows—and knows *not* to say. (There are social groups whose tactlessness is indulged, even hailed, as "telling it like it is"; children are among them, as are jesters and the very old.)

Yet if my tactless gesture harms not just one figure but the social order itself, the reverse is also true: as I shield the other from a harm that I could rightly inflict, I also work to keep intact the social process in which the two of us are taking part: a seduction, for example, or playing catch.

Or—to pick a site that helps us back on our path—doing therapy. Psychoanalysis is an undertaking in which meaning is produced not by one or the other actor of the therapeutic scene, but by the two to-gether. What is more, it is an undertaking that acknowledges this fact. In this respect, it is an unusual science. In other sciences, the object is taken to be as void of meaning as the orbit of a planet, which makes the observer into the sole source of meaning. Or else the object is seen as a bottomless well of meaning, and the observer is the mere amanu-ensis who labors to bring it to the surface (hence the faux-humility of critics and scholars). In psychoanalysis, however, meaning making—interpretation—is frankly participatory, which is why it can come about only with tact.

The critic Jonathan Elmer helps us see how in psychoanalysis inter-pretation links to participation. His point of departure is the work of the child analyst D. W. Winnicott, known for singling out the impor-tance of what he calls transitional objects, objects to which children attach a primordial significance—a blanket, for example, or a piece of string. These objects—or rather the child handling them—must be treated with great care, Winnicott counsels:

> Of the transitional object it can be said that it is a matter of agreement between us and the baby that we will never ask the question: "Did you conceive of this or was it presented to you from without?" The impor-tant point is that no decision on this point is expected. The question is not to be formulated.[15]

"The question is not to be formulated." We know why Winnicott feels the need to issue such a bald prohibition: it is because the question *can* be formulated. In fact, it *was* formulated just two lines earlier, by Winnicott himself. And we know that as a matter of rational inquiry it has standing: for certain purposes, it can, it *must*, be formulated. Which is why tact is called for.

Though as analyst or scientist or critic I am entitled, I decline to ask the baby if she conceived of her plush toy or if it was presented from without, and I do that to keep from harm the playing child and also the play world itself. In that world, the toy just is the thing with which the child plays. It's a dinosaur that has lost a savage battle to an elephant and is now licking its wounds. Was the dinosaur made by the child or in China? The world in which dinosaurs and elephants do battle has no room for such a question, and raising it is apt to spoil this play world. "The important point is that no decision on this point is expected."

If instead I ask what led the animals to quarrel or, saying nothing, get on the floor with the child, then I put myself in position to drift into playing. Without needing to forget that I am an analyst or scientist or critic, I become a player: an analyst-player, a scientist-player, a critic-player—one who takes part in the play world rather than taking it apart.

The key insight here is that playing with the child and making meaning with the child do not pull away from one another. They happen together. They happen together not just in child psychology or psychoanalysis, but anywhere meaning emerges in an encounter, which includes all criticism worth its salt. Elmer makes this point well. He shows that the Winnicottian ban on tactless questioning need not be confined to transitional objects or even to all playthings but can be generalized to hold for anything that can become an object of criticism. "The question of the relation of the creative and the critical," he writes, "of that which brings newness into the world—*poiesis*—and that which works on what is found in the world"—criticism—"may benefit from not being broached at all."[16] The question is not to be broached because the poetic has no room for it.

A German officer supposedly asked Picasso, "Did you make this?"— pointing to *Guernica*, the painter's mural about the bombing of the Spanish city by German forces—only to be answered, "No, you did." Picasso's response is often taken as insisting that his art is rooted in historical reality, which is, finally, a banality. In fact, his retort does something more powerful: it lays bare the blithe tactlessness of the officer's remark. The question of whether *Guernica* was conceived of by Pablo Picasso or presented to him by the Luftwaffe benefits from not being broached, not because it is incoherent or illegitimate (the officer may well have had good reasons for asking, just as a scholar or critic might), but because a decision about it must remain suspended in the world in which an encounter with the painting makes sense.

The arrival of the Wehrmacht is as good an occasion as any to acknowledge that tact, like every ethos, is embroiled in an ambiguous ethics; after all, it unfolds in the morally ambivalent setting that we call the world. Tact, I said, enjoins me to work to care for the social process, not to harm it; it urges collaboration. But we know that there is collaboration and collaboration, that good collaboration can mutate in the blink of an eye into complicity with a foe. Often, it is hard to tell the two apart. Perhaps real harm does come from reading the works of

Ferdinand Céline tactfully (that is, collaboratively); perhaps the same is true of writings by Mark Twain and Philip Roth and Henry James and Sigmund Freud and ... I may participate in a work only to discover that it has abused my engagement or even betrayed it (something that tends to happen to readers of stories by Heinrich von Kleist).

If I let myself be seized by the worry of becoming complicit, if I try to stay on the safe side, then—well, what are my options? I can break the social process rather than safeguarding it. I can opt to become "critical" and shield myself from the call of that which I read; or I can refuse to read; or ban books and burn them.

But I can work to suspend the worry of complicity. Do I then not risk finding myself hand in glove with evil? That is a risk, but the greater hazard, I feel, is being trapped in Manichaeanism, that reign of moral panic that shadows all actions, very much including the nonactions prompted by tact. One thing that the intimacy with poetic works reveals is that being vulnerable to their significance is not the same thing as being complicit with a system of meaning. Not all participation takes the same form or carries the same moral value. Just because something comes to matter to me poetically (or playfully), I need not be answerable for it morally or politically.

Poetic criticism urges an ethics of care, then not because it can be sure that poetic works are always worth caring for, nor because this care makes the world a better place. Neither of these is given. It is because poetic criticism supposes there is value in keeping at bay the pressure of moral conformity. This supposition it shares with other forms of work—psychotherapy, for example, and, to a lesser degree, pedagogy. Teaching, learning, doing therapy, hearing and speaking poetically—these are forms of caring that risk getting involved with the wrong crowd.

PLAYING IT BY EAR

Let's circle back to Roland Barthes. Do these reflections about tact encourage a new interpretation of *Empire of Signs*? They may, yet if that were all, it would be a paltry reward. They do more than that: they open a new way of relating to the text. Instead of supplying me with yet more things to say, tact teaches me to hold my tongue. Questions at its very tip, ready to roll off, go unasked: Did you conceive of "Japan" or was it presented it to you from without? Is this poetry or is it philosophy? Art or criticism? Description or interpretation? And so on. There is no exhaustive list of questions to be avoided, just as there is no definitive guide to tactful behavior. That makes mastering tact tricky. What may be said and what may not changes with the situation: asking about the relationship between "Japan" and Japan is sometimes out of the question; sometimes fine; and then, sometimes, a must. There is no categorical imperative of tact. You must play it by ear: there is no rule to follow, just a tune or a beat. We are back with *Taktgefühl.*

"Playing it by ear" foregrounds the important idea that criticism worth doing—poetic criticism—is governed by no method. But there are other ideas dwelling in the background of the phrase. Five are worth spelling out.

First, playing it by ear requires that I *play*. When I play, I *do* something, I bring forth something. That simply makes explicit what we have known all along, namely, that the silence in tact is pregnant: it engenders speech (or music, movement, conviviality, or some other poetic act) that is attuned to the rhythm of the work coming before it. *Not* broaching the question of where the poetic stops and the critical begins is not a mere omission: it opens the way to thinking together—no: to *practicing* together—the poetic and the critical. It brings about a form of making: poetic making.

This form of making—the second background idea concealed in plain sight—involves (or just is) play. I play at criticism. Do I then play the way I play with the child and her injured dinosaur, or the way I play catch or play Scrabble? These ways of playing differ widely, but they all share one feature: they require the player to take part. To play, I must take part. If I refuse participation or take part half-heartedly, then I am a spoilsport: I spoil not just my own part in play but the entire play world. Being tactful may express itself in reticence, but that is not the same thing as remaining aloof; tact—and criticism attuned to it—obliges me to take part.

Third, taking part means having a part: having a part in the sense of having a role to play, but also in the sense of not having it all nor being all there is. By taking part, I acknowledge that I am partial, that I speak not from a place of detached sovereignty, but from within a situation that exceeds me. That is true even when I play alone: when I am riffing on a guitar in the privacy of my room or when I have the toy to myself, I take part in a public world, a world with a history and a grammar that comes before me and continues after me. Which is why tact commits me to the social world. Poetic criticism has society built in.

The fourth idea follows from the first three: if playing is a mode of making, and if this mode is not self-sufficient but participatory and partial, then playing must be attuned to the workings of another agency. Hence the need for an ear. I listen to the other, I take in the other, I study the other, the way players in a jam session or in a pickup ball game monitor each other for changes in tone or tempo.

Tucked inside is another idea, which is so parasitic on its host that it does not merit its own number. It is this: the form of attunement involved in acting tactfully—in playing it by ear—entails the full panoply of cognitive and emotional skills. This might seem glaringly evident, yet even discerning observers overlook it. Jean-Paul Sartre, among the few philosophers to give tact his attention, recognizes that tact requires the skill "to appreciate a situation at a glance." Yet immediately his left hand takes back what the right hand has given. He diminishes the skill by stripping it of all access to rationality: to take in a situation at a glance turns out to mean no more than "to feel it rather than to analyze it"; it turns out to mean that the one acting with tact has a conception of the world "for which *he can give no reason*."[17] It is a thought so manifestly wrongheaded that one wonders if only philosophers are at risk of holding it. Just because with tact feelings are in play, analysis and reason need not be absent. On the contrary, they must be present: if we observed someone acting tactfully, and they could give *no* reason for their behavior, we would rethink our assessment. Tact is, as Gadamer writes, also a "mode of knowing." Playing it by ear demands finely tuned modes of observation and evaluation.

Finally, the fifth idea to be brought into the foreground: if tact is participatory, and if it requires modes of observation and analysis, then these modes, too, must be participatory. Hence, once again, the aptness of playing it *by ear*. The ear is an organ that is always open, that remains exposed to outside stimuli. Willy-nilly it takes part in what it monitors. When my response to a work is guided by tact, when I play my criticism by ear, then I do not scan a situation "from without," as Winnicott put it; I do not probe or judge it as a detached observer would. I take part. And I scan, probe, and judge (if I do judge), the better to take part.

Scanning, probing, and judging: do we mean anything more by criticism? Criticism and participation, we now see, need not be opposed. Quite the contrary: they go astray when, prodded by mistrust, the one is pitted against the other. Criticism that seals itself behind a glass wall interrupts the play of meaning making. Rather than continuing, it aims for conclusion: it seeks to have the last word, not because it brooks no dissent, but because its idea of interpretation—to bring to light what the work holds within it—entails the idea of an end of criticism. Once the meaning has been exposed, there is no more to say. If criticism keeps being produced, it must be because up to now the meaning has not been extracted completely enough.

Poetic criticism, by contrast, is open-ended: it continues where the work leaves off, and it is to be continued. Which is why no criticism—no work of any kind—is poetic when it is born but becomes poetic only when it has prompted another work to come into being. The critic Andrew H. Miller calls this form of criticism "implicative" (and contrasts it with "conclusive criticism"): it implicates the reader in the performance of its own thinking, doing what it can to elicit a reply.[18] In the terms I have been using: it invites—it urges—the reader to take part, and it does so because this criticism itself takes part in what it criticizes.

Participation has hooks on both ends: it attaches to what comes before and it affords occasions for future linkages. Because its form of interpretation takes part in the work rather than remaining aloof from it, poetic criticism remains vigilant to Benjamin's idea that art is "merely a transitional stage" in a process that leads to criticism. Yet this criticism, in turn, is merely another transitional stage leading to another manifestation of the poetic: to art or criticism or social action or a meal, each a leaf floating atop the stream of generativity.

POETIC MAKING CONSERVES AS IT RENEWS

Tact, I said, takes part in a process rather than taking it apart. It shelters the process from harm. Its ethos aims at care, and its goal—one goal—is to safeguard. To the degree that it works to keep intact what it handles, tact is conservative. And because poetic criticism requires tact, it too is conservative.

It is this conservatism of tact that draws the attention of both its advocates among scholars and critics, the few there are, and its many detractors. Take Hans-Georg Gadamer, perhaps the most prominent of advocates. His hermeneutic theory strives for "the rehabilitation of authority and tradition," and so he understands tact in a way that furthers that aim.[19] "One can say something tactfully," he writes, "but that will always mean that one passes over something tactfully and leaves it unsaid" (15). That is congenial with what I have been saying: to shield the social process from harm, tact remains silent about what could, truthfully, be said. Now note where Gadamer takes this thought:

> But to pass over something does not mean to avert one's gaze from it, but to keep an eye on it in such a way that rather than knock into it, one slips by it. Thus tact helps one to preserve distance. It avoids the offensive, the intrusive, the violation of the intimate sphere of the person. (15)

Tact is watchful "in such a way" that it sidesteps collisions and preserves distance. It promotes delicacy and decorum. It teaches manners.

It is just this maintenance of convention, so valuable to Gadamer, that leads most theorists and scholars to dismiss tact (should they take note of it at all). When Theodor Adorno meditates on "the dialectic of tact," he sees in it nothing but an agent keeping in place conventionally established "inhuman conditions." In fact, it is worse than that, for tact upholds a convention that is

> no longer intact yet still present. Now fallen into irreparable ruin, it lives on only in the parody of forms, an arbitrarily devised or recollected etiquette for the ignorant, of the kind preached by unsolicited advisers in newspapers.[20]

Not enough that tact is conservative; its conservatism is of a grotesque kind, for what it seeks to embalm has long since wasted away. Tact plays the part of the conservationist in an open-air museum of oppression.

It is true that tact can foster conformity. Tact is also not the sole way of doing poetic criticism, and not every social process merits participation, nor every person or object care. There are reasons I may not wish to respond to a work such as *Empire of Signs* by playing along. I may feel bullied or exasperated by its tone, or too tightly implicated in its embrace. Sometimes poetic criticism calls for other moods and other modes of behavior. Still, I don't want to give up on tact too quickly. Not because I wish to defend conventions (though, where would we be without them?), but because tact is richer and deeper than the skill, prized by Gadamer, that "preserves distance" and "avoids the offensive," richer and deeper, too, than the "arbitrarily devised or recollected etiquette" brushed off by Adorno.

Return to the child playing with the dinosaur. When I get on the floor to play along, there are things I say and things I pass over, things I do and things I don't. I do try to avoid "knock[ing] into things," to use Gadamer's words, but does that mean I work to "preserve distance"? On the contrary: I work to establish enough intimacy to slip into the play world. Does my behavior avoid "the offensive, the intrusive, the violation of the intimate sphere of the person"? Probably, yet it would be odd to say that my behavior *aims* at avoiding offense. Being polite is not my goal; rather, I am trying to play with the dinosaur and the child, and I do what I can to nourish this playing. Usually that will involve not giving offense, but sometimes the dinosaur may need to be put in his place, or the child and I may, through our toys, get entangled in fighting, or we may accuse each other of cheating, which itself could be a game. There are ways of giving offence that can end play, and there are ways that promote it.

Just because tact sometimes aligns with politeness or decorum does not make them the same. There are social processes that I safeguard precisely by being boorish or combative. Roughhousing, taunting, and trash-talking may not be good examples of etiquette, but they are good examples of tact, though we do not often use the term when describing them. They require real aggression, but aggression applied in precise enough doses to remain just this side of open hostility—tactful aggression. Or take sexual play, where harm and care end up in the tightest and most confounding of embraces. Being tactful in sex may involve smutty talk; it may involve humiliation or the threat of violence or even real violence. This can go wrong, but if the vulgarity and the aggression are whispered in the right tone, if the violence is just violent enough, then sexual play is nurtured and intensified: just watch *Gilda* and listen to how Rita Hayworth leans into Glenn Ford and breathes the words "I hate you too, Johnny. I hate you so much I think I'm going to die from it," before the two melt into a kiss.

What has this detour revealed? Tact, we now see, is conservative to the degree that it conserves a social process. This process may be conventional and ossified (and hence blameworthy to those who frown on the status quo), or it may be guided by the authority of a tradition taken to be legitimate (and hence praiseworthy to thinkers such as Gadamer). In both cases, it is geared to the preservation of a past order.

But its opponents *and* its defenders acknowledge only a segment of the much larger region of behavior that tact governs. Preserving the past need not be its sole orientation. It can also work to sustain the vitality of the social process in which it is engaged: to conserve the forward momentum of the process and its progress into the future. Here, the conservative dimension of tact cannot be extricated from its progressive dimension, since the one reinforces the other: the more I steep myself in a process, the more I am inclined to safeguard it, and the more I commit myself to safeguarding, the more I find my way around the process, which also means finding ways of playing in and with it, of taking it in directions and giving it forms that, while prepared for by the past, remain unanticipated by it. That can happen in child's play; it can happen in sexual play; it can happen while doing improv or doodling or writing criticism.

It would help if we had a word that captures this mode of mindful participation; decorous tact would be a mere species of that genus. Lacking such a term, I stay with "tact" and stress its musical meaning: a sense of tact allows me to feel and then to follow the beat in a song, but also in a piece of writing, a film, or a situation. Rather than tying me to the weight of etiquette or of tradition, this tact frees me to play things by ear.

Let's spread out what we have before us so we can pull it together once again. Poetic criticism, I said, is poetic because it brings forth more poetic criticism (whatever form that may take). I read Barthes on sushi, and it makes me want to write. The basic gesture of poetic criticism is not to bring the process of reading and writing to a close, but to further it. A response is not preoccupied with the past alone: yes, it responds to a call that preceded it, but then, ideally, it becomes itself a call for a future response. To pull this off, poetic criticism needs tact, I also said. Tact urges the suspension of certain questions and judgments to permit me to take part in a process. Its basic orientation is participatory.

Now the filiations of these lines of thinking begin to reveal themselves. Tact allows me to take part in a process in a way that, while not arbitrary, is infinitely open. When I participate, I give myself over and let myself be led, yet in such a way that the range of the moves I make can surprise even myself.

POETIC POWER

Once more, then: poetic criticism takes part; it is partial; it is participatory. To be participatory, it requires tact (in the term's wide sense) and it requires intimacy; it was intimacy, after all, that led us to tact. But is all this participation, this tact, this intimacy not too close for comfort? More relevant to scholars and critics: is it not too close for knowledge? Does it not obscure knowledge or even blot it out entirely? If scholarship and criticism aspire to more than opinion mongering, if their aim—at least one aim—is to get at the truth (which, roughly put, is the point of the knowledge of science), then they must remain wary of a way of speaking and behaving that risks concealing the truth. Does the free exercise of the inquiring mind not entail a disregard—a contempt even—for niceties that get in its way? "I am attracted by the notion of a hearty indifference to one's own and other people's feelings, when a fragment of the truth is in question," the critic and poet William Empson has rousingly written.[21] Should we not all feel this attraction?

Tact maintains a complicated relationship to knowledge—I have admitted as much. Facing the naked truth, tact sometimes averts its eyes from what is in plain sight; sometimes it avoids saying what it knows cannot be denied. To a champion of the truth, that can look like timidity; it can look like complicity cowering behind the screen of politeness. If *Wissenschaft* is your game, then any dithering when even "a fragment of the truth is in question" will seem like betrayal. Still, if, with Winnicott, we insist that certain questions are "not to be formulated" (again, with the understanding that these questions do not belong to a fixed canon, but change with mood and situation), then we grant that poetic criticism, like Winnicottian psychotherapy, will sometimes forgo interrogating the work or the child, even when the questions might add to knowledge. In poetic criticism, there is, then, something more important than the knowledge science seeks.

What is this something that outweighs knowledge? And what kind of knowing is it that poetic criticism passes over in silence? We know the answer: the something that is more important than securing knowledge is the social process that tact shelters from harm and thus makes available for participation, and the knowledge being avoided is the kind that would harm the social process. This form of knowledge is not merely negative, an interruption of the process or its derailment; its negativity yields something positive. This is less mysterious than it may sound: we know that harming the social process can be generative. Recall Paul de Man's dictum: "A mood of distrust produces rather than paralyzes interpretive discourse."[22] It does, and not interpretive discourse alone: while it blocks the path to participation, distrust enables detachment, observation, analysis, critique—in short, the whole kit and caboodle of scientific work, including the work of the sciences of literature, history, art, and the other humanities. That is old hat.

But passing over some forms of knowledge does not mean that poetic criticism is mute about all knowledge. What is more, it is only by passing over knowledge that poetic criticism has a chance at the more important task of disclosing the truth. There is a truth that reveals itself in intimacy, through tact, and in participation.

Take an ethnographer, for instance.

> She has spent more than thirty months in the Bocage in Mayenne [in Western France], studying witchcraft. "How exciting, how thrilling, how extraordinary ..." "Tell us all about the witches," she is asked again and again when she gets back to the city. Just as one might say: tell us tales about ogres or wolves, about Little Red Riding Hood. Frighten us, but make it clear that it's only a story; or that they are just peasants: credulous, backward and marginal. Or alternatively: confirm that *out there* there are some people who can bend the laws of causality and morality, who can kill by magic and not be punished; but remember to end by saying that they do not really have that power: they only believe it because they are credulous, backward peasants.[23]

Jeanne Favret-Saada opens her account of witchcraft—of being "caught" by witches and "uncaught" again by unwitchers—with a familiar geographic conflict. Witchcraft unfolds in the country, yet its ethnography belongs in the city with its scientific institutions. The story stands in for the clashes that shape her book: credulous native informant versus academically trained ethnographer; fairy tales versus the laws of nature; magic versus science. The notion of a "clash" does not do justice to the relationship of the two sides of the conflict, for they do not meet on equal footing. Rather, one side, namely science, which is the side that frames the conflict in the first place, seeks to govern the other: the ethnographer sets out to expose the secrets of the native informant; the laws of causality do permit witchcraft, but only in fairy tales and superstition; and magic exists as long as it aspires to being no more than a bag of tricks explicable by science.

It is true that ethnography is not literary studies. Still, in this conflict, Paul de Man would be at ease on the side of science: its vigilance—its distrust—keeps the researcher from being taken in by the doings of the natives, leading to the production of an "interpretive discourse" capable of withstanding scrutiny.

The trained ethnographer knows what is expected of her: to translate the experience of the countryside into the language of the city, to turn fieldwork into science and superstition into knowledge. That is standard operating procedure. Favret-Saada zooms in on the degree zero of the ethnographic method, the very point at which an occurrence becomes "field work," which later, in "the city," metamorphoses into science.

To do ethnography, the ethnographer requires information. Where to obtain this information? From informants, of course; that is why ethnography has had to conjure them. Informants inform, and they inform by speaking. "To be an ethnographer," Favret-Saada writes, "is first to record the utterances of appropriately chosen native informants" (9). Words are spoken; they are recorded; they are copied and recopied, arranged and edited; they are parsed, catalogued, and interpreted; and after much massaging, they find their place in an account that arrives with a claim to being knowledge. It arrives with a claim to have found the true meaning of the original words.

Again, doing ethnography is by no means identical to doing scholarly work on literature or film or visual art, but—and here is my brief for staying with this ethnographer of witchcraft for a bit longer—when the work is formalized at an abstract enough level, the homology becomes apparent: words, found somewhere, are transformed, in a laborious process requiring much skill and knowledge, into other words that announce the true meaning of the first words. It is what ethnographers do, and it is what we scholars and critics do.

Favret-Saada thinks that, when it comes to witchcraft, this interpretive method of transforming raw information into ethnographic knowledge fails, and we think we know why. We suspect that something must go awry somewhere in the long chain of recordings, translations, and transformations that link the words coming out of the informant's mouth to the words the ethnographer puts in her book, the way a message is inevitably mangled in a game of telephone. If the flaw were in the relay system, there would be hope that with enough care, with enough distrust, skill, and knowledge, we *could* get the method right. But that is not so. Favret-Saada's finds the rot deeper down, at the very source, with the very words of the informant. She gives us the how and the why in a passage that must jolt anyone grappling with works of art and works of reflection:

> Now, witchcraft is spoken words; but these spoken words are power, and not knowledge or information.
> To talk, in witchcraft, is never to inform. Or if information is given, it is so that the person who is to kill (the unwitcher) will know where to aim his blows. "Informing" an ethnographer, that is, someone who claims to have no intention of using the information, but naively wants to know for the sake of knowing, is literally unthinkable. For a single word (and only a word) can tie or untie a fate, and whoever puts himself in a position to utter it is formidable. (9–10)

Witchcraft is spoken words; but these spoken words are power, and not knowledge or information. That is the heart of it. It is why an informant informing the ethnographer about witchcraft never tells the truth, even when sincere.

But most informants are not sincere and have no reason to be: if words are power and not knowledge or information, then someone arriving all the way from Paris asking about witchcraft cannot possibly be asking for the sake of idle curiosity, as she avows; she must be up to *something*. "So long as I claimed the usual status of an ethnographer," Favret-Saada recalls, "saying I wanted to know for the sake of knowing, my interlocutors were less eager to communicate their own knowledge than to test mine, to try to guess the necessarily magic use I intended to put it to, and to develop their force to the detriment of my own" (11). In a state where "total war is being waged with words" (12), there is no impartial use of words. There is neither information nor knowledge unless it serves power. There is no idle chatter, for, as the ethnographer learns, chatter itself is a form of tactical warfare:

> It conveys to one's interlocutor that one might launch a magic rocket at him, but that one chooses not to do so for the time being. It is conveying to him that this is not the time for a fight, but for a cease-fire. When interlocutors for whom witchcraft is involved talk about nothing (that is about anything except what really matters) it is to emphasize the violence of what is not being talked about. More fundamentally, it is to check that the circuit is functioning, and that a state of war does indeed hold between the opponents. (10)

In a situation of total verbal combat, an ethnography that relies on information to arrive at knowledge misses the truth of witchcraft, and misses it completely. It ends up knowing *nothing* about witchcraft—in fact, less than nothing, for it fools itself into believing that its research into the age, gender, and social status of witches and unwitchers, into the number and kinds of their interactions and the grammar governing them, must have revealed something. But it understands nothing, because it looks for information where it needs to feel the power of words.

Therefore, Favret-Saada concludes, "one must make up one's mind to engage in another kind of ethnography" (12). One must walk right into the two snares that all ethnologists have been trained "to avoid like the plague: that of agreeing to 'participate' in the native discourse, and that of succumbing to the temptations of subjectivism" (23). These supposed snares turn out to offer the only way forward:

> For anyone who wants to understand the meaning of this discourse, there is no other solution but to practise it oneself, to become one's own informant, to penetrate one's own amnesia, and to try and make explicit what one finds unstatable in oneself. For it is difficult to see how the native could have any interest in the project of unveiling what can go on existing only if it remains veiled. (22)

It is one of the virtues of Favret-Saada's book that she keeps her eyes fixed on witchcraft and avoids general pronouncements even in her reflections on knowledge, truth, and method. That allows her readers to reach for thoughts that they take as their own, when in fact she has prepared the ground. If you are a scholar of literature, then the first

such thought is: is what she says of witchcraft not true also of literature? If a philosopher, then: is it not true also of philosophy? And if
an art historian or film scholar or musicologist, you wonder: is it not
the same with art or film or music? Is it not true in all these areas that
the sources—the native informants—never provide just information
that can serve as the raw material for scientific or scholarly knowledge,
but always also engage in combat or flirtation or deception or flattery?
(The second thought that occurs is whether not all forms of human
communication behave this way.)

You realize that poetry (and philosophy, painting, film, music) is a
form of witchcraft, requiring another kind of criticism, one that seeks
the truth that poetic making reveals, rather than some knowledge it
might glean by asking questions and taking down answers. For "there
is no other solution but to practise it oneself, to become one's own informant, to penetrate one's own amnesia, and to try and make explicit
what one finds unstatable in oneself."

Recently scholars have been insisting on the knowledge and truth
in criticism; they have sought to ground literary studies in "a disci-
plined set of procedures for the production and transmission of knowledge" and have bolstered the discipline's claim to "critical truth."[24]
Favret-Saada permits us to see that you are barking up the wrong
tree if you hope to emerge from an encounter with poetry or with
witchcraft in possession of some quantity of knowledge or of truth. At
best, you come to wield poetry or witchcraft and in that way acknowledge their power and their truth. What matters is acknowledgment:
poetic criticism—like magic, like sorcery—is a way of acknowledging
the truth in the power and the urgency of words (and not of words
alone).

Stanley Cavell has observed, "acknowledgment goes beyond knowledge," not in the sense of being more or better knowledge but "in its
requirement that I *do* something or reveal something on the basis of
that knowledge."[25] Saying that the call issued by a poetic work incites
a response grasps just this requirement that I do something, which is
what takes acknowledgment beyond knowledge. When I hear a call,
"it is not enough that I know" what the call says, "I must acknowledge
it," I must *do* something about it, "otherwise I do not know what [it]
means" (263). Understanding the poetic work entails more than understanding what it says.

PHILOLOGICAL DISARMAMENT

To find poetry in poetry, you must hear and speak poetically. That is what Friedrich Schlegel, the inventor of the term "poetic criticism," teaches. "Poetry," he writes in a fragment, "can only be criticized by poetry."[26]

For a while now, I have thought that the line says all one needs to know about poetic criticism, what it is and how to do it, and that it therefore requires neither commentary nor critique. It is clear as day, and yet, like so many of the best aphorisms, the clarity slips away as you reach to grasp it. It is an enigmatic clarity. Is that why I keep returning to it? Or is it because I keep failing to find the right way of hearing it and responding to it? If I knew how, then it would stop coming back to me, and before long I could forget it. Criticism thinks of itself as memorializing a work, but if it is done right, then it is a way of ingesting and metabolizing the work and, finally, of discarding and forgetting it.[27]

"Poetry can only be criticized by poetry." It is a plain phrase, yet right away I feel the urge to poke and prod its every part. Can I be sure what it means by the word *poetry*, if *poetry* is even the right translation of *Poesie*, or if the first usage of the word denotes the same as the second? As Schlegel uses the term elsewhere, *poetry* is not restricted to a genre such as the lyric, nor even to verbal works in general, but reaches for the essence of creative making, whatever form it takes. Does that hold here? Then there is the word *only*: am I to take literally the assertion that poetry can be criticized by poetry alone and by nothing else? Now I notice the passive voice and find myself asking by whom—by what unnamed agency—it can only be thus criticized? And what of this criticizing? The word itself—*kritisiert*—rankles, as does the idea it evokes: does poetry stand in need of being criticized?

The fragment goes on: "A judgment of art that itself isn't a work of art . . . has no right of citizenship in the realm of art." "A judgment of art": a phrase I have come across a thousand times, yet only now do I hear how off-key it sounds, how grating it is to join "judgment" to "art." Worse, this "judgment" is apt to give the aimless drift of associations stirred up by "criticize" a Kantian bent. And suddenly all I am able to see in "criticize" is "critique," that prosecutor that summons the accused before the Tribunal of Reason to press them for answers. Before I know it, an air of anxiety has settled over the line, and rather than enjoying the cloudless simplicity it had once offered, I become restless and turn over each of its words.

But why such unease? I approach the phrase as though in it I confront a being that speaks an unintelligible idiom whose meaning requires decipherment, when instead I could begin by crediting its affinity. It is, after all, not very mysterious: "Poesie kann nur durch Poesie kritisiert werden." "Poetry can only be criticized by poetry." The words show the way, more clearly, by a stroke of luck, in the English translation, which begins and ends with "poetry": poetry is where I set out and it is where I land, my dwelling and my destination. Though I may not know its dimensions nor the measure of its boundaries, I face in it not an alien object, but something with which I maintain an unknown intimacy. Often, I approach it as though it were an obscure substance to be probed with the stick of scholarly analysis, but then I forget that I know it from inside, even when its words confound me—forget that, *because* I know it from inside, its words confound me in the way that poetry does.

Having intimacy with it does not mean that it harbors no mysteries; I have said that. It means that poetry is not an object to be studied, dissected, and decoded. It is, in fact, no object at all. That, too, is something the line intimates: when poetry encounters poetry, the two do not occupy opposite poles—here I, the reading subject deploying "poetry"; there a poetic object that I approach and whose meaning I seek to parse—with critique or criticism coursing between us. If criticism itself is done "*by* poetry," as Schlegel puts it, then poetry is the medium through which I move, not a thing I hold before me.

Even the term "medium," recruited to dissolve the dyad of subject and object, will not quite do. It fails to capture the strange affinity I have with poetry—and it with me—if I am to hear it in the right way. For poetry is not a medium in the sense of a means, not a tool I wield or a channel I select to tune into a special form of communication. Nor is it a medium in the more capacious sense of a setting, the stage of my actions or the stream that carries me away. In either case—whether I hold it or it holds me—it remains alien to me, something I think of as belonging to the world rather to myself. Yet to do criticism *by* poetry names something more intimate: a form of comportment, an ethos.

HEARING THAT WE MAY SPEAK

We scholars have been reading this fragment (along with other writings in the archive of "Early Romanticism") as a building block in an intricate theory of literature, when in fact it is a call to action. It presents us not merely with new thoughts, but with a demand. It asks us to "hear, that we may speak," as Emerson has already told us.[28]

Do I need to learn how to hear and to speak? Do I not do it in my sleep? Of course I do, but that is just the reason Emerson urges a different mode of hearing and speaking. Every day, language passes through me without leaving a ripple. Yet from time to time I come across words, and something happens. The words snap me out of my slumber and suddenly I hear in them a call that asks something of me. No longer do I read to add to my stock of interpretations; I read, rather, to take part in a form of making. I remain vigilant about the ways of seeing—the theories—that the text unveils, yet mainly because they can lead me to new ways of doing. Rather than leaning back, content to behold the shape they reveal, I change my posture and lean forward, ready to learn how these words set in motion something in me.

That is the dimension of urgency in poetic criticism. It manifests itself once intimacy allows me to face the work, disarmed. Rather than bringing about a placid concord with the work, intimacy exposes me to an intensity that urges a change in me: I experience it as a call, a quickening, a tension, a force whose meaning often remains obscure, yet whose reach I cannot elude.

So: I hear Schlegel's words that I may act. The way of acting toward which they guide me is clear. I am to encounter poetry with poetry, to act poetically when coming across poetry, where poetry—again—is not a special category of artful writing (lyrical, complex, sophisticated—what have you) but names ways of making that outstrip communicative use—ways of passionate making or urgent telling that you also encounter in necromancy, in augury and voodoo. The fragment asks me to face the coming into being of something new, not with the aim of fixing its location in a grid of meanings, but rather with a gesture that launches my own ways of making. If criticism names the encounter with the poetic, then a real encounter, and real criticism, must itself be poetic.

How do I bring about such an encounter? The fragment does not say. Yet, in whatever way I go about it, my work—criticism—no longer remains the same. It ceases to serve as the mere occasion for assigning praise or blame, nor does it document an arrangement of meanings derived from, or imposed on, a source. Something different happens.

For one thing, something *happens*. In poetic criticism, someone speaks. Someone ventures an act of speech—an act *in* speech. Even if it has been uttered before, such a speech act is unheard of. Ideas that have grown flaccid gain fresh vigor, like a muscle that one learns to feel anew. Yet this speaking, though new, does not emerge out of thin air but follows upon another act, an act of hearing—hearing *this* fragment by Friedrich Schlegel, for example—an act as fragile as the speech to which it gives rise. For to hear "that we may speak," to hear poetically, demands of me that I open not my ears alone, but also my self, that I allow myself to be exposed to what speaks to me, unshielded by my usual armaments—with effects I cannot foresee. Learning to become vulnerable in this way lies at the core of encountering poetry with poetry. It is the urgency born of intimacy: only when I have some intimacy with it, do I become vulnerable to the urgency of an utterance or act.

What changes, then, what is at stake in hearing the fragment, is more than criticism. If I succeed in hearing the poetry in some arrangement of words (just as I might perceive it in a composition of images, sounds, or movements), then they rouse me from the torpor of my habits and bring to consciousness ways of encountering things that had lain dormant. My whole organism comes alive, and as I learn to hear and see and feel anew, fresh possibilities of making sense of the world reveal themselves, which turn out to be just fresh possibilities of making the world. That changes everything. More than anything, it changes me, for now I must become someone able to be roused from his torpor.

This is the dimension of reading in which the text speaks to me, touches me, and ultimately changes my place in the world. It is a moment of interpretation, but one we tend to misrecognize, since the roles have been reversed: rather than my having something to say about the work, it is the work that says something about me. The way it speaks to me and activates something in me is essential to my being able to say something about it.

The idea that I myself must change to be capable of certain experiences (not quite the same as the idea that I must change myself) is

similar to the ancient notion that a subject must undergo a transformation to receive insight and knowledge. In this conception, knowledge
is not a possession that the subject amasses but a challenge it must
accept, a call to reshape itself to be able to receive knowledge—to be
worthy of the knowledge that it is making its own. But there is also a
difference: in the encounter with the poetic work, the method and
process of transformation is not one I fully master. There are bodies
of knowledge I can acquire and techniques I can learn. Often, they aid
me, though sometimes they get in my way (and I never know which
of these will occur).

But they can never prepare me for the moment a poetic work addresses me in a way that surpasses my capacities, the ways it touches
a wound I did not know I carried. Which is why the change brought
about in a poetic encounter cannot be folded into a system of education—a project of *Bildung*.

SECOND THOUGHTS

Have I been reading too much into this line by Schlegel? Does it really
say that poetry is not an object nor I a subject, that hearing it involves
knowing it from inside, that its urgency issues from the intimacy I
have with it? If so, how and where? Fair questions. Still, it's irksome
that they interrupt our reverie. Was not the idea to keep at bay the
unease that our usual modes of reading have taught? Yet here I am,
ready to shadowbox with challenges of my own making. And once I
start, there's no stopping: behind these questions a hundred others
lurk, each ready to take a swing. Strange that ease does not come easily. Second thoughts molest me before I have come to know the first.

But is ease a state I have ever possessed? If so, I would have hope
of regaining it by calming the agitation that has taken hold of me. Yet
nothing I know from experience or history lends weight to this supposition. There does not seem to be a primitive condition, in our own
childhood or in the "childhood of humanity," in which human beings
enjoyed a calm that was later disturbed by psychic and social tumult.
Even infants are plagued by disquiet. (They aim to soothe it by dreaming up games like fort-da, Freud tells us.) Tranquility, it seems, is something to be attained, not something to be retrieved, since the most stri-

dent voices reverberate in our heads. Plugging our ears does not silence those voices, far from it; it permits them to echo more violently.

The lament about first and second thoughts may have it backward: what are called second thoughts in fact beset me first. I start with a head full of noise and get some peace when the quarrelsome voices have lost their edge. It is then that they can tell me something worth hearing.

In attempting to hear Schlegel's fragment or any poetic configuration, I cannot, then, simply shrug off challenges issued by philology, by history, or by critique, hoping to return to a state of mind unmolested by questions, for I never knew such a state. Instead, the way of making I seek is also a way of relating to knowledge—knowledge derived from philology, history, critique, and other sources—that allows me to find words that are a match to my experience.

SELF-REFERENCE VERSUS URGENCY

Back to Schlegel's fragment: how do I know that I am to read it poetically? Who tells me that I must lean in to hear it, that I must know it from inside? The answer is trivial: the text itself does—who else? But not by forking itself in two, one part raising itself above the other and from its meta-perch speaking about the one below. There is no *about*, no cleavage between words as ideas and words as instructions for how to read ideas.

Though spelled in the same letters and composed of the same words as a prosaic proposition, the poetic utterance speaks in a different manner and solicits a different way of hearing. That is true not of our fragment alone but of every poetic act, no matter its form or medium. It arrives with a force that infuses seemingly ordinary signs with the peculiar urgency that solicits a distinct comportment.

That sounds more mysterious than it is, for it is known to anyone who has come face to face with a poetic act. It is exactly what the narrator of Elena Ferrante's novel notices about her brilliant friend, Lila:

> Not only did she know how to put things well but she was developing a gift that I was already familiar with: . . . she took the facts and in a natural way charged them with tension; she intensified reality as she reduced it to words, she injected it with energy.[29]

We learn a few things here. One is that Lila's ability "to put things well" is distinct from, perhaps even unrelated to, her gift of intensifying reality as she reduces it to words. Poetic intensity may go together with "putting things well" (a "good style"), but it needn't, and often it doesn't.

There is another insight the passage offers, and it is this: in intensifying words (and signs generally), the poetic act intensifies the very reality it has "reduced . . . to words"—"reduced" in the sense not of diminishment but of concentration to an essence, as when a sauce is reduced to become a pure agent of flavor. In fact, a poetic act is most successful when it arrives as an intensification of things rather than of signs (though we scholars, believing we have discovered the true location of poetry, do not tire of scrutinizing these signs). The poetic intensity of a Lucian Freud portrait makes itself felt in the reduction of the human figure to something more essential than any face or torso one may encounter, just as the poetic force in the play of Lauren Bacall's eyebrows is seduction reduced to an elementary and potent distillate.

It is true—trivially true—that the fleshiness of Freud's figures is made up of patches of color and that Bacall's erotic edge is an effect of the way she arches her brow and turns her head (and of countless other techniques that come together to yield her image on screen); that is where artistry lies. The poetry of the act, however, flashes up *in the things*, and if we fail to feel the tension in those things, the examination of signs remains blind in one eye; it lacks a dimension.

Poetic acts come about when words chafe at the conventions of meaning and release enough energy to bring forth the very things they designate. (Words stand in here for all the ways of acting poetically, despite their differences.) They arrive with a tension that shakes off their ordinariness and charges them with unforeseen urgency. Like a power surge, this urgency leaps from words to things and lights them up.

The tension is not always easy to notice. Some texts—Schlegel's fragment is an example—keep their readers so busy with the mysteries of the propositions they contain that it takes time before their poetic energy is felt. Their prose works like bait that distracts from their poetry, where "poetry" and "prose" name not genres but degrees of vibrancy: what is conventionally labeled prose at times pulsates with a poetry lacking in much of what is called lyric poetry—open any page by Kleist or Conrad, Nietzsche or Emerson. ("One writes good prose only *face to face with poetry*," Nietzsche says.[30])

There is another thing, at least as significant, that we learn from this page in Ferrante's novel: the surge of urgency from signs to the things they signify is not the endpoint of its spread. Look how the passage goes on:

> ... she intensified reality as she reduced it to words, she injected it with energy. But I also realized, with pleasure, that, as soon as she began to do this, I felt able to do the same, and I tried and it came easily. This—I thought contentedly—distinguishes me from Carmela and all the others: I get excited with her, here, at the very moment when she's speaking to me.

"As soon as she began to do this, I felt able to do the same." We know what "this" and "the same" mean here: they name the poetic act, the vivacity that leaps from signs to things. Now we come upon another vector of poetic contagion: the shudder that intensifies reality also passes from maker to onlooker and turns *her* into another maker, and thus a new source of transmission.

Is it that simple? For some apparently it is; the narrator "tried and it came easily." For others the path is steeper; "Carmela and all the others," those nonbrilliant friends, seem to belong here. If poetic making comes easily to Ferrante's narrator, it may be because she has a more direct access to the source: she gets "excited with her, here, at the very moment when she's speaking to me," while the rest of us must rely on an intermediate station on the trajectory of this communicable condition, namely, the work.

But perhaps that is not right. Perhaps directness is overrated. Perhaps the work, that reduction of the flavors of reality, delivers a greater punch than the maker does in her full presence. It may be—sometimes, for some people—that urgency, defying the laws of the material world, *gathers* in strength as it travels from maker to work to onlooker.

Where has this detour taken us? To a region both familiar and strange. In asking how the poetic nature of a fragment by Schlegel—like that of any work—communicates itself, I did not take up the idea of self-reflection, whose warrant is issued by Romantic writers (Schlegel among them) and taken up by scholars and critics. It consists of the idea that an act of communication is refracted through some device—a mirror, a false bottom, an ambiguity, an opposition, a frame that twists what it holds—and that this refraction is where the poetic lies, for it doubles and, hence, exceeds the "straight" picture of things. Against this idea, which takes communication as the transmission of quanta of meanings (albeit meanings split into distinct yet interfering channels), I found myself drawn to the idea of communication as urgency—as the transmission of intensities.

EPIPHANIES

So: rather than speaking with a forked tongue, Schlegel's fragment puts words together in a way that pushes them beyond themselves. Their demand to be heard poetically is an urgency, not a proposition. It is experienced as "an epiphany of knowing something through words that could not be put in words."[31] That is John Williams writing in *Stoner*, a novel generous with such epiphanies. Can one quote an epiphany? One can try. Here, William Stoner, the protagonist, has just met a young woman called Edith, and the narrator takes a moment to tell us about her upbringing:

> Her childhood was an exceedingly formal one, even in the most or-dinary moments of family life. Her parents behaved towards each other with a distant courtesy; Edith never saw pass between them the spontaneous warmth of either anger or love. Anger was days of courteous silence, and love was a word of courteous endearment. She was an only child, and loneliness was one of the earliest conditions of her life. (54)

This is a world in which absence holds immeasurably greater power than does presence—a world dominated by the gesture that is refused, by the word that remains unspoken, by the sibling that never arrives. What is withheld overwhelms what is given. Sometimes it seems as though what is given, rather than having its own solidity, manages no more than to make palpable—achingly palpable—the weight of that which is withheld.

That is true of the novel too. It is littered with invisible words, black holes that bend the visible words out of their usual course. And just as black holes in outer space become noticeable not directly, but by refracting light coming from other bodies, so too the silences in the novel make their massive absence felt by torquing words into telling shapes. For example: between the sentences that convey the aloofness between the parents and the final sentence of the passage—

> Anger was days of courteous silence, and love was a word of courteous endearment. She was an only child . . .

—there is just a period, but the space it takes up is vast and dark. It divides two situations: On one side, there is a marriage built around distance, in which the couple circle one another in fixed, icy orbits, always in sight but never getting close. Then, abruptly, Edith appears in her loneliness. We, readers, can perhaps cope with each of these situations, but how do we cross the space between them and get from the marriage to its offspring? How does the pair's lovelessness beget the loneliness of the child?

If the narrator withholds the transition we crave and abandons us to ourselves it is not because he is coy or passive-aggressive. He would be if he were keeping to himself some morsel of intelligibility that might appease us. But is it intelligible why a child, conceived in love making, inherits the parents' inability to love? It happens all the time, we know, but that does not make it easier to comprehend how one generation transmits its sadness and cruelty to the next. The opposite is true: that it happens all the time—that it is inevitable, or nearly so—is exactly what makes it so hard to comprehend.

Like every tear in the fabric of meaning, this incomprehensibility is difficult to bear, and we desperately seek to mend it with verbiage borrowed from psychology and sociology. The narrator of *Stoner* takes a different route. He braves the pressure to speak and to soothe. He remains silent, not because he has nothing to say, but because the very absence of speech is an acknowledgment: it acknowledges that the urge to fill the hole in comprehension with an abundance of words— enough words to cover a whole life—can only go unsatisfied. His silence does not issue from reticence or reserve but is a tongue-tied silence: words press forward yet fail to articulate. They are too much and not enough.

It is a strange thing, then, this silence between sentences: a way of "knowing something through words that could not be put in words," but *without* the words—an epiphanic silence.

Since we are here, we should note that epiphany is not the only mode in which poetic urgency makes itself known. Look at what else goes unsaid in the passage. The narrator does not say—because he need not say—that William and Edith will marry; the moment she walks into the story, we understand that they will. Nor need he say that the coldness that is her patrimony will, inevitably and incomprehensibly, enter William's life and chill it to the marrow. That, too, is something we come to know through words, though it cannot straightforwardly be put in words. Yet this way of knowing does not arrive with the sharp slap of an epiphany. It takes time to gather force, like the pressure that builds before a headache. These silences do not hide in specific places but permeate the passage. They are dreadful; they channel dread.

The flare-up of an epiphany is one form urgency takes, but there are less flamboyant, though no less intense, forms of knowing something through words that could not be put in words: a heaviness or a lightness (anguish or joy, for example), vertigo, perplexity, wonder, laughter, and many more.

Sometimes, reading or rereading *Stoner* or Schlegel or other works, these forms of urgency are easy to pick up, and sometimes they go unnoticed. Some of it has to do with the conventions of reading: *Stoner* stands in a tradition of writing that encourages readers to listen for certain things (silences, for example), while Schlegel's fragments fit no genre and so leave readers at sea. But these conventions can only do so much. If I am in the wrong mood or have a tin ear, then I fail to hear the urgency, as in other contexts I might miss the flirtation or reproach in a phrase, and even the most meticulous analysis of the words cannot make up for my deafness. Now the words are no more than instruments, inert signs pointing at things, and because pointing is such a tricky business, I soon find myself entangled in decipherment and fretfulness.

If instead I manage to pick up the poetic tension, I begin not by staring at a linguistic puzzle but by hearing a voice whose texture I know even when I fail to understand all it says. I stop pretending that I am confronting a message composed in exotic symbols that must be worked out bit by bit, like a signal from a distant planet. There is some intimacy now, and intimacy brings ease. I can spare myself the agitation that comes from pursuing the endless lines of meaning that slice through every utterance, nor do I need to play the game of one-upmanship that marks interpretive traditions, from the Talmud to deconstruction. I exhale and start letting down my guard.

But with the ease of intimacy comes vulnerability, and vulnerability can bring unease, of a sort different from the commotion caused by textual decomposition. The unease born of intimacy is more unnerving. Because the words and the silences that puncture them emerge from close quarters—because I know them from "inside"—they can get under my skin and hit a nerve.

THE INTENSE LIFE OF LANGUAGE

The philosopher Gaston Bachelard may be thinking along these lines when he writes that "poetry puts language in a state of emergence." How to picture this state? Here is how Bachelard develops the thought:

> The poetic image is an emergence from language, it is always a little above the language of signification. By living the poems we read, we have then the salutary experience of emerging. This, no doubt, is emerging at short range. But these acts of emergence are repeated; poetry puts language in a state of emergence, in which life becomes manifest through its vivacity.[32]

The passage begins where we too find ourselves, namely with the mystery at the heart of the poetic image: poetry partakes of language, and yet stands apart from it. To grasp this excess relative to the ordinary language of naming, Bachelard, like so many other thinkers, reaches for a spatial image in which poetry "is always a little *above.*" We picture language separated into layers, the poetic layer floating atop the signifying layer like oil over water.

But then he catches himself, drops the spatial image, and switches to a temporal logic: he asks us to *live* the poems we read, and thus to live the emergence from language. Poetry now does not hover over ordinary language, regarding it from above, but names the metamorphosis of the ordinary. If reading a poem is living a poem, then the poetic emergence from language is not a release from language; it offers no escape into ineffability or wordless ecstasy. This emergence from language, this intensity that shakes language loose from its encrustations, occurs *in* language.

Poetic acts, we now see, rather than splitting language in two, effect a transformation within language—a transformation *of language by language.* Which just means that poetry is not something that enters language from outside (thanks to a muse, for example), nor is it a specially marked region of language, "parasitic" on its "normal" uses, as philosophers of language and linguists often assert.[33] It is, rather, one of the things you do with words. Poetry reveals itself as a force that language holds in reserve, allowing it—*compelling it*—to emerge from itself. Hearing the poetic edge in language is hearing language as though it had not been heard before.

Has the mystery of poetic speech been lifted? If you are of a scholarly or scientific disposition, then hardly, for in that case you wish to know what, precisely, propels words beyond their practical utility into the orbit of poetry. What does that force consist of and how does it unfold? You would be in your rights to ask for a catalogue of features that characterize the state of emergence, the better to identify poetry. When Bachelard then offers the thought that "poetry puts language in a state of emergence, in which life becomes manifest through its vivacity," you cannot help but be disappointed. Do we know how life manifests itself in its vivacity any better than we know how language manifests itself in poetry? It seems that one mystery—that of poetry— has been replaced with another—life.

Yet we might also be led to a different insight. Instead of feeling let down by Bachelard's failure at providing an explanation, we might wonder what an explanation of poetic urgency could look like. Are we even in need of explanation? Is poetry? The texture of Bachelard's meditation—the fact that it *has* texture—reveals that I cannot learn to grasp the force of poetic words by launching a theoretical investigation. I come to see, rather, that the account I give of the way I read poetry— the account I give of living it: call it criticism—must itself occur in language that is in a state of emergence: it must be poetic.

Schlegel's fragment says nothing more than what Bachelard's words show. One way of criticizing poetry by poetry is to say that in the poetic image "life becomes manifest through its vivacity." A scholar or scientist might, in another bout of scruples, insist on a list of features that characterize life (metabolism, reproduction, and so on), which would then be used to judge every case that presents itself. Yet to say that life manifests itself through its vivacity simply means that life can only be known through life, as poetry can only be known by poetry. It is another way of saying that urgency makes itself felt in intimacy.

There is another turn worth following. Life, we begin to see, does not merely serve as a model for poetry. Poetry showing itself through the intensity of language is not *like* life showing itself through its vivacity. No, the very way life manifests itself through its vivacity comes about in the intensity of poetry. The quickening we feel in poetic intensity *is* a manifestation of life in its vivacity. "These linguistic impulses," Bachelard continues, "which stand out from the ordinary rank of pragmatic language, are miniatures of the vital impulse"—the *élan vital* made famous by Henri Bergson, whose vitalism Bachelard sees everywhere in poetry. The *élan linguistique* is not a sign—a representation, a metaphor—of the *élan vital* but one of its instances. If we learn to see "language-as-reality," rather than "language-as-instrument," then Bachelard promises that we "would find in poetry numerous documents on the intense life of language."[34] Here, then, is another nondefinition of poetry: language lived through its vivacity.

WHAT AND HOW

Language-as-reality. What of this "as"? When we think of words announcing themselves "as poetry," we risk thinking of them as engaged in impersonation. But words do not lead a quotidian existence that issues into poetry through an act of masquerade. The conjunction "as" yields another form of doubling, distinct from the self-reflection that Walter Benjamin and others have noted in the Romantic conception of the work of art, yet as likely to lead us off track. It opens a rift between words and poetry just where we want to feel their intimacy. Bachelard, too, seems to be led by this intuition, which is why he speaks of *langage-réalité* and *langage-instrument*, leaving as little daylight between the terms as he can get away with. (The connecting *-as-* insinuates itself in the English translation.)

If instead of asking how words appear "as poetry," we wonder how they come to speak poetically, then we nudge ourselves in the right direction. Now, we are more likely to see that poetry is neither an object nor a phenomenon, not a being to which I can point. Its center of gravity lies not in a noun, but in an adjective or an adverb. It is not "poetry" we seek, then, but rather the manner—the style—in which a word, a gesture, or a motion comes to make itself felt poetically.

Okay, but does that need to be said? Do I not know already that I must look to the *how* and not the *what*? Of course I do, yet strangely this way of knowing seems to maintain its claim on me for only as long as my gaze is fixed on it, and no longer. The instant my mind wanders, the insight, which moments before had the clarity and cogency of self-evidence, slips into obscurity, and as I lose my grip on it, I reach for the solidity of nouns to steady myself: I talk of "poetry," its features, its history, its influence, its effects, its essence.

The habit is hard to break, but at least I come by it honestly, for I have learned it from philosophers and critics, Friedrich Schlegel among them. To be fair, many of them do mention the *how*, but usually the way one recommends a dish for its nutritional benefits. Their duty discharged, they proceed to feast on a rich spread of *whats*: on "poetry," "art," "literature," "the absolute," "the work of art," "the beautiful," "the sublime"—each concoction more elaborate than the next, each requiring years of exacting training to construct and assess.

As so often, the master showing the way is Plato, whose signature skill lies in turning adjectives into nouns. By asking what the beautiful dress, the beautiful horse, and the beautiful face have in common, with each other and with all other beautiful things, he means to direct our attention from surfaces, which, by his lights, shimmer with illusion, to the essence of things, imagined as resting in a remote region, shielded from change.

Plato has the integrity to admit failure—at the end of the *Greater Hippias*, the dialogue devoted to discovering what makes beautiful things beautiful, we find Socrates empty-handed—yet this failure turns out to bear more fruit than most successes do. Now there is something called "beauty" to be accounted for, unseen yet ubiquitous, manifest in countless shapes yet unchanging, an entity filled with metaphysical mysteries in need of examination and explanation, which a long roster of keen minds strives to supply: philosophers, theologians, poets, rhetoricians, historians, psychologists, anthropologists, sociologists, biologists, and many others. (The most recent to try their hand are neuroscientists, as devoted to the laws of beauty as any Platonist, except they seek to find them etched not in immutable tablets handed down from the realm of ideas but in the soft tissue of the brain.)

It is true that in Plato's writings "beauty" maintains no especially close link to "poetry" or to "art." Only centuries later will these concepts be woven into a network that in the Western tradition is called aesthetics. Yet when the network emerges, its nodes are understood by aesthetic theorists according to a Platonic model, even by those theorists who decline to carry the full weight of Plato's philosophy. The perplexity at the heart of poetic experience is made to disappear with an elegant act of metaphysical legerdemain: the poetic force of words is taken to be caused by their "poetry," the *how* by a *what*. (Nietzsche debunks the process by doing what good debunkers do: he shuts out the magician's patter and keeps the eyes fixed on his hands. An expert demonstration of this technique can be observed in the first few pages of his essay "On Truth and Lying in a Non-Moral Sense.")

THE KNOT OF EXPERIENCE

The poetic is the *how*. It is how language-reality emerges from language-instrument. Yet in reaching to become more familiar with this *how*, we keep grasping at *whats*. That is not a simple error but the knot at the core of poetic experience.

We won't be able to undo this knot, nor would we wish to, for then the experience itself would unravel. Yet we can follow the twists and turns that make up the knot, the better to see what kind of grip poetic experience has on us.

The first twist of the thread seems to pull away from the objective world and into subjectivity. That is because of the sort of thing a poem—which just means: any poetic work—is. And we know what sort of thing: it is a singular thing. But singular in what way? Is the poetic something utterly new, something never before seen or heard? Yes and no. An image, a phrase in a work of reflection (take Bachelard's), the pause an actor makes in delivering a line—when they arrive with poetic urgency, then I am led to think that they have not been written or performed before.

But their novelty is not exhausted by the fact that a new phenomenon has appeared on the horizon. A solar eclipse or a stock market crash too may be singular: it may be true that in our lifetimes there has not been an eclipse or a crash quite like *this* one. Yet the event has not thereby become a poetic singularity, and not because eclipses and crashes are not poetic or artistic, but because a poetic singularity cannot appear in a general guise. Acknowledging it is not a matter of scientific verification or collective consensus. This includes a scholar's assurance, backed by historical evidence and formal analysis, that some phenomenon—Schlegel's fragments, say—breaks new ground. The scholar's insight may even persuade me, but unless I make it my own, it is just something I read in a book. The poetic must not only have been *made* singularly, but also *experienced* as having been made singularly—here, now, by me.

What if I miss the poetic force that others have felt in a work, because I am distracted or a dunce? That happens, and it would be my loss. I may feel shame for having failed where others have succeeded, yet I would be mistaken to conclude that what continues to elude me is something hard and real whose presence could be demonstrated by objective means.

The idea that aesthetic experience remains deaf to the force of concepts is not new; it lies at the heart of Kant's aesthetic theory. "If someone reads me his poem or takes me to a play that in the end fails to please my taste," Kant writes, then I am moved neither by famous critics trying to sway me nor by rules that supposedly govern a successful work. Quite the contrary:

> I will stop my ears, listen to no reasons and arguments, and would rather believe that those rules of the critics are false or at least that this is not a case for their application than allow that my judgment should be determined by means of *a priori* grounds of proof.[35]

Coming upon this one image—Immanuel Kant himself plugging his ears against arguments, an obstinate child shutting out the voice of reason—is fair recompense for the hours spent navigating the long, cheerless corridors of the *Critique of Judgment*. But its drollness should not mislead us about how far-reaching the idea is for the enterprise of criticism. Criticism that operates with "reasons and arguments," Kant is saying, has no authority over aesthetic experience—*none*. The reasons may be airtight or specious, and the arguments well supported by evidence or not: it makes no difference. My experience may be enriched by this reasoning, but it will not be "determined."

By the same token, a piece of scholarship that places a work in a conceptual frame—a historical trajectory, a genre, a philosophical proposition, a political program, a social tendency, a technique—can be right only at the cost of crushing what is poetic in a poetic work. Which means that most of what passes for critical scholarship of poetic works (literary studies, art history, film studies, musicology, and so on), whatever else it does that might be of value, misses the poetic core of those works.

The thought may seem insurrectionary to professional critics. Everyone else knows that if I fail to pick up the poetic force of a work because I am inattentive or tone-deaf, then no amount of formal or historical analysis can make up for this deficit, just as a meticulous study of the words someone has uttered is unable to disclose their seductive or sarcastic overtones.

Following the thread leading into the knot seems to have landed us in the thick of subjectivity. Now it sounds as though the poetic is whatever I say it is. Is that what I am saying? Again, yes and no. Acknowledging the force of the poetic cannot happen in general, not in the "we" of science, scholarship, or common opinion. To acknowledge the poetic, a sharply contoured "I" is required. This "I" need not be confined to an individual: the audience in a theater, the crowd in a stadium, or, indeed, We the People of the United States, seeking to establish a more perfect Union, can become such an "I."

But the poetic has not thereby become arbitrary. Led by a flight of fancy, I cannot simply declare a thing poetic and be done with it. That is because the experience of poetic singularity—and here is another loop in the knot—is not mine alone, walled off from others by the boundaries of my person, by my particular tastes and distastes. In its very makeup and quite apart from my intentions and my place in the social order, it opens to others and calls on others. Society is woven into it. The experience is social, and essentially so, even if it takes place on a desert island or in the solitude of my skull.

We must understand "social" in the right way. My experience of the poetic is not social in the sense that it must align itself with the acclaim of others. Its validation lies not in market value or in market share. Nor is it social because it typifies a social position. Poetic experience exceeds the well-defined markers of my "identity" (my class, my nation, my sexuality, my geography, and the rest).

It is true that my experience cannot help but emerge from the welter

of ways of knowing, feeling, judging, making, acting, speaking, imagining, daydreaming, even hallucinating that have pressed on my life. And
how could it not? "There is no delirium," Gilles Deleuze has written,
"that does not pass through peoples, races, and tribes, and that does
not haunt universal history."[36] What goes for my feverish reveries also
goes for my experience of the poetic. Yet to be haunted by history and
to haunt it does not mean that my experience adds up to the sum total
of historical forces and no more. It means, rather, that, having passed
through them, it surpasses them. The experience registers the singularity of the poetic just when it lays bare not the commonalities of shared
life but the impersonal in my person, the place where an opacity keeps
me distant from my quotidian self.

We have been tracking the loops in the knot of poetic experience. Has it brought us anything but more entanglement? Recall
how we came upon the knot. We said that encountering the poetic—
"criticizing" it, as Schlegel likes to say; hearing it "that we may speak," in
Emerson's words—has a shape that differs from my experience of ordinary objects. To hear and feel the poetic impulse—the *élan poétique*—
means hearing and feeling things in a way that takes them beyond their
ordinary ways of signifying and functioning. Familiar things now have
an urgency that jolts them out of known circuits of meaning and into
something unknown, something singularly new. That was our first
description of the knot. In following the thread that leads into it, we
were led from objectivity into subjectivity—from an account of the
singularity that would characterize the poetic thing to the singularity
with which I receive it. Then we saw how this subjectivity loops back
out of the subject and opens to the public.

But we have not gone in one end of the knot only to emerge from
the other into the same objective world. Rather, the way my experience
of the poetic relates to the thing I encounter and to myself deforms
the concepts of objectivity and subjectivity beyond recognition. We
are better off without them, since they lend a false familiarity to what
is unfamiliar. Kant's notion of "subjective universality" is an attempt
at capturing this dimension of poetic experience with received philosophical terms. Its ungainliness acknowledges what Kant's analysis of
aesthetic judgment reveals, namely, that in these judgments both subjectivity and universality are profoundly altered. Is a subjectivity that
is "not grounded in any inclination of the subject (nor in any other

underlying interest)" still worthy of its name?[37] And what about a universality so toothless that it can only issue demands for assent without means of enforcing it?

Kant has zeroed in on a region of experience, flagrant in the encounter with an aesthetic object, where the subject, by reaching a point that exceeds subjectivity, achieves a negative universality. It is the same point Emerson has in view when he says of the poet that "the deeper he dives into his privatest, secretest presentiment, to his wonder he finds this is the most acceptable, most public and universally true."[38] The knot, then, does not lead us out of the dimness of subjectivity back into the daylight of the objective world, but urges us further into knottiness, a place where I no longer feel my known self but, to my wonder, find something public and universally true.

MAKING FREEDOM

The poetry Schlegel has in mind, the poetry to be criticized and the poetry criticizing, is not exhausted by markers of genre or convention, I have said, not confined to lyrical or elevated language. It is a more general phenomenon. In one of his lectures, Schlegel describes it as a kind of thinking. "There is . . . a kind of thinking that produces something," he notes. He calls this productive thinking "the making of poetry [*das Dichten*]," which "creates its material itself."[39] Understood this way, the key characteristic of poetry is not beauty, not truth, not pleasure, but a creativity in thinking. Creativity must then also be the mark of any form of criticizing that wishes to maintain its citizenship in the realm of art.

But why prize creativity? Why pursue it? What does creativity create? When you learn to hear that you may speak, what do you say? Well, many things. The themes, methods, and goals of criticism practiced in Schlegel's or Emerson's vein are endlessly varied, as are its forms. Your speech may be verbose or terse, high-flying or modest. Or it may cease. What you hear may so dumbfound you that you fall into muteness. Yet, however varied content and form may be, your speech—your silence included—is a poetic act.

That may not sound like much, but if you pull off such an act, then—besides whatever "content" or "message" your act may hold—you have

enlarged the space of what you allow yourself to say or to do. You surprise yourself. You do something that you did not know you knew how
to do. This bit of extra elbow room gives you space for new ways of
acting (toward others, toward things, and toward yourself), ways you
could not have foreseen. It is a form of freedom: moving without the
encumbrance of fear and without, therefore, the need to defend what
has not even been attacked.

Now the world has become wider and deeper. This enlargement
does not merely augment the known world but changes its makeup.
For you have done more than to add this one new possibility of speaking and acting stimulated by a solicitation; what has been introduced
is the very possibility of proliferating the possibilities that the world
affords. True, the quantum of new wiggle room may be minute, in itself hardly momentous; in the grand scheme of things, how significant
could the words be that you utter in response to the fragment? Yet your
actions betoken a profound freedom. For with even the humble poetic
act you alter the very texture of the world: it is no longer simply there
as the sum of what presses on you and what must be administered. No
longer are you limited to responding to demands issuing from the envi-
ronment, as animals do, or as we imagine animals do. The world turns
out not to be exhausted by what is given but is immeasurably enlarged
to include what it *could* become, and become through your doing.

It is true that a poetic act—hence also poetic criticism—is not a
practice; never will it be entirely governed by a theory or shoehorned
into a method, for something in this way of doing surpasses the capacities and competences of a subject. Still, poetic making is not counter-
feit making, as philosophy keeps charging.[40] Its way of making is as
real as any action. In poetic acts, the world, and not its semblance,
is transformed. In this way, the world reveals itself as something you
can form. (If you are a Heideggerian, you might just say: it reveals
itself, period.) Even if you manage to vary its shape by only a small
degree, bending a corner here and flexing an edge there, you face a
world whose physiognomy has softened: what was once an unyielding
arrangement of circumstances beyond your reach, you now find to be
pliable—something given, yes, but given to be made.

What is more, the freedom to make something of this world—the
freedom to say and do what you did not know could be said and done,
which is the freedom to make poetically—this freedom does not rest

in you as a silent reserve (a "natural endowment") into which you may tap as needed, nor has it fallen to you by chance. It is also not the freedom of speaking or doing that a sovereign has bestowed on you; if challenged, it would not help holding up a bill of rights. The freedom in Jackson Pollock's drip paintings, the freedom he felt in his bones and the freedom the paintings still unleash in others, is not there ahead of time (in the form of codes or rules, spoken or unspoken) but comes about in the very making.

In shaping the world in some way—putting together words or sounds or gestures "in which life becomes manifest through its vivacity"—you make not only some object but also the freedom needed to make that object. You surprise yourself with what you have done, with the fact of making: before doing it, you didn't know it was permitted or possible. This is a fragile freedom; it may not survive the work. It cannot be codified. It was not there all along, a pocket of vacant space of defined dimensions waiting to be occupied but has come into being thanks to an act of poetic making.

And that is not all. It can happen that when you manage to hear and to speak—*if* you manage—others hear your words, and hear them that *they* may speak. So you surprise not just yourself but others too, me perhaps, spurring me to make my own elbow room, by my own lights and in my own way. Because *you* acted more freely, *I* feel freer. And vice versa: my move might in turn rouse others (you, why not?) to attempt their own moves, and before long the freedom to make the world has spread like a contagion of fresh possibilities.

One key difference between this poetic freedom and the liberal kind now reveals itself. Liberal freedom is mutually restrictive: my freedom, fully exercised, limits yours, which is why my freedom must be constrained. Likewise, your freedom must be curtailed to safeguard mine. But in poetic freedom the opposite is true: your freedom enables and encourages my freedom. In this way, it is infectious—it moves laterally, opportunistically, like sorcery.

Granted, this freedom that transmits itself from work to work has an odd form, as odd as the form of the poetic response that gives rise to freedom and, somersaulting, is enabled by it. This is not the freedom of the will that we know from practical philosophy; it is not "the will's property of being a law unto itself," as Kant puts it at one point.[41] The freedom in poetic making does not enjoy the privilege of autonomy, for there is no law that it might give itself. If I am to respond to poetry poetically, then I can rely on no principles or techniques to bring about my response reliably and methodically. The experience will always elude my full grasp and remain out of reach of my concepts.

Despite the language of making that we have resorted to in these pages, poetic making is a way of doing but not a practice. It is not open to the sort of analysis and description that admits replication, the sort Aristotle undertakes in his *Poetics*. Rather than me bringing it about, I feel it as something that befalls me. It is a way of being I neither manufacture nor simply suffer. In it, I feel the delicious freedom *not* to exercise my autonomy, a freedom from the burdensome freedom of my will.

Acting poetically is contagious, then, and what communicates itself from utterance to utterance is neither a message nor an idea but a way of relating to the world and to myself, and it is this that provides the sharpest thrill. For only in the actions of others does it dawn on me that I myself have acted, and not because they "reflect back" to me what I have done. If I found in others merely what I knew from myself, I would feel flattered, no more. But I find instead that they have taken my act—my words—in their own way rather than mine, just as I used Schlegel's words for my own purposes rather than his. They hear in my words a voice other than the one I know, and it is in these departures that I may see how, when I acted, I too ventured—or just stumbled—into a new situation. It is in acknowledging what is alien to me in what others have done that I am apt to gain an intimacy with the stranger that I am to myself.

This operation of venturing something new, of crossing an unknown limit, of making a move unforeseen by the rules of the game, though mute about the situation to which it leads, discloses a world more capacious than it was, replete with latent possibilities. The act reveals this world as waiting to be woken, receptive to being formed, and reveals me as capable of bringing about this forming. This change in the aspect of the world, coupled with awareness of a freedom to bring about this change, a freedom I did know I possessed, does not leave me cold, however precarious such freedom may be. I salute it and celebrate it.

Not that the world suddenly smiles upon me with sunshine and birdsong; I have not entered Arcadia but remain in the world I know.

Yet in it I face something new and inviting, a structure both supple and open. It is a richer place now. And though I know that it may become richer in ugliness and wickedness just as much as, or perhaps more than, it does in beauty and benevolence, I also know that this even-handedness looks for the poetic difference in the wrong places. Calling the world rich does not result from tallying gains against losses. (Do I even know how to calculate the outcome of a single poetic act, let alone to reckon several acts against one another?) Its richness emerges rather from the fact that the world becomes the staging ground for my acts.

Responding to poetry with poetry; hearing that we may speak; feeling the vivacity of language—these gnomic formulas reveal themselves as ways of reaching for the same idea, embarrassing almost in its plainness: they urge me to say something that might startle me with its newness. And, again, this urgency lies not mainly in the message they carry, in a request or exhortation, but in a language charged with enough intensity that it throws off sparks, which, with luck, kindle poetic acts in those gathered around them.

This leads to another nondefinition of the poetic: poetic acts do not just bring forth products; they are rather acts that, in bringing forth products, bring forth other poetic acts. Poetic criticism is not a mode of speaking and writing that makes assertions about objects; rather it is a mode of speaking and writing that, in making assertions, engenders more criticism. You know the feeling: you read an essay or just a fragment, and you feel urged to sit and write. You write not to play up or play down what you have read, nor to amplify or object, but because something you read—the twist in an idea or an adjective that had no business being there—woke something up in you.

"Books are the best of things, well used; abused, among the worst," Emerson writes in the essay we have been going back to. "What is the right use?" he asks, and provides his own answer: "They are for nothing but to inspire." And just as we are getting comfortable with the thought, reaching for the pencil to mark it, he adds: "I had better never see a book, than to be warped by its attraction clean out of my own orbit, and made a satellite instead of a system."[42] The pencil hesitates. Are we ready to undersign this last thought? Have we not said that we go to books to lose our way and not to keep to the path? When reading a book, do we know when we are satellite and when system?

Now we see that we have let Emerson's line warp us clean of our orbit and put us on a satellite's course, even though he has just told us its right use. We read to be inspired. If that is too mawkish, then say: we hear so that we may speak. And if that sounds too oracular, then: we read—we look, we listen, we feel—to do things we did not know we could or would or should do. Or just: to make freedom.

PART 3

But I Don't Know How

(OPACITY)

One last time, then:

> Something speaks to me.
> I must tell you about it.
> But I don't know how.

The varieties of being spoken to and of telling, I've said, are endless, but so are the varieties of not knowing how: I think something has spoken to me, but I cannot be sure; I don't know how to hear what is said; or when I think I have heard, I don't know what to say, or from which place to speak (in which tone, style, voice, volume); or I find a way but don't know how I got there (cannot retrace my steps); or I worry about speaking too quickly and fixing the wisps of feelings and intuitions into propositions and judgments that I am then stuck with. Or I think I have nailed it but find you looking bored or baffled, which makes me wonder about the nailing.

The image of the three-step offered itself many pages ago. It emerged from an experience, common enough, in which the encounter with a significant thing—my starting point was a passage from a novel by Franz Kafka—takes shape by passing through three moments: something arrests my attention; I feel pressed to act on it; then I discover that I am not up to it—I find myself stymied, or else I am conspicuously voluble, or I take cover behind the paraphernalia of my profession. The image has had its use, but now, contemplating the final step, I worry it might take me off track.

Looking at the varieties of not knowing how, even the few that came up right away, I note that opacity is not a step I take *after* I have gone through intimacy and urgency. It is there from the very start. If we are to imagine it as a step, then it is a third step that shapes the two preceding ones completely, like in a waltz where, besides the forward momentum—step 1 leads to step 2, which in turn gives way to step 3—there is also a reverse causality: the promised arrival of step 3 forms step 2, whose anticipation gives the shape to step 1. It was the temporal order of actions (which include non-actions like remaining silent) in the encounter with Kafka's novel—*first* . . . , *then* . . . , *then* . . .—that led me to the image of steps, yet it is no more, but also no less, than an image. Which just means: sometimes it fails to reveal a feature of the phenomenon whose intimacy I am seeking, and sometimes it shows me more than the case warrants. Since there is no perfect image for something that, like opacity, does not fully yield to being imagined, I will need to bring others into play, aware that sooner or later every image lets you down.

SHADOW IN PLAIN SIGHT

I don't yet know much about this not knowing how, how to describe it or what to make of it, but I can say this: opacity is not something added to intimacy and intensity, which is why I cannot subtract it to possess them pure and simple. It is not an optional ingredient of the experience I have with poetic works, which can be works of art or works of reflection or works of other kinds. Not knowing how belongs to intimacy and urgency like—another image—the shadow belongs to the illuminated body.

And how does the shadow belong to the body? The way an effect belongs to a cause: the contact between light and a solid body brings about a shadow—the illuminated body is the cause, its shadow the effect. The shadow is simply a segment of darkness—nothing fancy, just the absence of light—fixed in its geometry by physical features (the size and shape of the body, the angle of collision with the light, etc.). I might seek the shadow cast by a tree or shun it, I might find it beautiful or frightening, yet I would not confuse the tree with its shadow.

Or would I? The laws of optics are one thing, but the way the world presents itself to me is quite another. Here the shadow maintains a greater intimacy with things than physics might allow.

Picture a drawing of a soccer ball—a plain circle filled with the typical black and white pattern. Now sketch a grayish patch somewhere below it, and right away the ball is no longer a disc on a blank sheet but a *ball*. It lifts off the page and into three dimensions; it might even feel like it has taken flight. This metamorphosis happens even though the gray patch makes no part of the ball's structure or substance—an everyday bit of magic. Since it is the ball we look at, we do not usually take in its shadow (nor the magic), but when it goes missing, we feel something is amiss. The shadow, then, is no part of a body's ontology, yet its absence leaves the body with a diminished reality. It both belongs to the body and does not belong.

Has this new image gotten us further? Not if we think that intimacy and urgency are solid like soccer balls and opacity an interesting smudge that accompanies them. But if we look at their relationship— the ways of belonging and not belonging—something about this mysterious phenomenon might reveal itself.

Look, for example, at the work of the visual artists Robert Irwin and Anish Kapoor, in some of which missing shadows—and the *way* they are missing—get at why the work feels so eerie. Every visual artist works with light and hence wrestles with shadows, but few work as diligently at keeping them at bay, not to vanquish them and assert the supremacy of pure illumination but, rather, to choreograph adventures in perception. Irwin fills large rooms with light so uniformly diffused that one gets the sense that the light has always been there and will always remain, the room's changeless, motionless content, like water in a fish tank. It comes from nowhere and aims at nothing, has neither origin nor direction, and for that reason casts no shadows. Since no room in this world looks that way, both the light and the room, which now is nothing but *space*, feel like they have been teleported to Earth from another world. You stand there, despite yourself drawn to this uninhabitable, impossible space, and you don't know whether to stay or to go.

Kapoor makes sculptures with concavities so flawlessly curved and surfaces of such velvety, hushed black that, again, shadows are given no chance. The eyes find themselves undecided: are they looking at three dimensions or two? Or some number in between? Circumstantial evidence points to three: you are quite sure that the cavity is no optical illusion and that you could, if the room monitor were not looking, stick your hand in. But as you gaze into the hollow of the thing (it is a thing, not a full-blown object), one of the dimensions keeps slipping away. And here is what is arresting about the episode: though your epistemology wobbles, the whole thing yields sheer, undiluted beauty—a moment of happiness, all the more exquisite for having come unforeseen.

One thing these sculptures by Kapoor have in common with Irwin's installations is that they defy being photographed. Is it that you cannot take a picture of something lacking a shadow? That would go along with what I've been saying. But then what about Andreas Gursky's 99 Cent, a bird's-eye photo of a 99-cent store taken from a perch just below the ceiling, where a security camera might hang?[1] You look and look and see nothing but merchandise encased in light, a light so absolute that it blots every shadow out of existence, revealing a weird and otherworldly space (though an otherworld different from Irwin's). Only later do you realize (because you have experience with such things or because someone has told you) that you have been looking not at one photo but at an exactingly polished composite of many: you see not what the store *is* but what it *should* be—the Platonic form of the 99-cent store—where not even the shadow of a shadow is allowed to becloud commerce. This, then, is not a picture of a world without shadows, but an unshadowed world made in a picture—more painting than photograph.

I come away with this: at first, it was the shadow's darkness that made it an apt image for opacity. And for good reason: opacity manifests itself in the folds of experience; it hides from reflection; it is obscure. Because it is difficult to get through a sentence about reflection without using the language of light (in the words of the philosopher Hans Blumenberg, light is an absolute metaphor), blocked reflection cannot help but appear as blocked light. Yet now we see that the obscurity in an encounter can exist in plain sight, see it in a way that is less open to discussion than knowing is. We see that there is more to shadows than darkness, and more to opacity than dimness of knowledge. We see—really *see*—the missing shadow, not because it has made an imprint on the retina (how could it have?) but in the way its absence sets the mood of the seen world. That is why this excess in illumination also appears as a blot on experience: the pitiless light of the 99-cent store makes it feel uninhabitable.

Opacity, then, can invade me under a clear sky, not despite but because of its cloudlessness. Irwin's light-flooded spaces and Kapoor's shadow-proof sculptures pull me in, as does the air-conditioned glare of Gursky's print. They urge me to do something, perhaps say something. But what? I don't quite know where to look or where to stand or what to feel.

Shadows make us nervous; we worry about ghosts lurking there. But spookier than shadows may be their absence. Where but in plain sight can ghosts hide in a shadowless world?

Some of what is true of the illuminated body is true also of the voice. I have heard it told that when phone calls were first channeled through fiber-optic cables, the conversations were so perfectly devoid of static that callers found them unnerving. Fearing the line had gone dead, they kept seeking assurance that the other was still there. To calm their nerves, the phone company added shadow to the voices, injecting the immaculate glass filaments with a gentle thrum: the callers' words, no longer swallowed by an unearthly void, took their place in a dimensioned, bounded space, a space textured enough to make room for an interlocutor. Their voices regained body and weight and resonance. We know that noise can be a voice's rival; it can muffle a voice or drown it out. Yet for a voice to have reality, this rival must make itself heard.

Likewise, opacity both belongs and does not belong to intimacy and urgency. It does not belong when the two are imagined as authentic only if they arrive in pure, spotless immediacy; anything less would yield degraded forms of intimacy and of urgency. This way of seeing things makes opacity into an alien thing that tampers with experience—a chronic hiss interfering with what speaks to me and with my speaking, one I'd wish to eliminate. Yet if we take intimacy and urgency not as ideal types but as existential modes of being, then opacity belongs to them as it belongs to all human life. Without this shadow, intimacy and urgency would have no reality; they would not be.

What have we done other than lurch from one image of opacity to the next? It is a *step*, we said, the last of three. —But that makes it sound as though it is something added to experience, like an optional ingredient in a recipe. —It is a *dimension* then, something intrinsic to the structure of the world; without it, we would have not a lesser world but no world at all. —Okay, but does opacity come in such geometric form? Is it not more of a stain in experience, a vague *shadow* getting in the way? —Were it a shadow, then it could be erased with better lighting, could it not? We could get rid of that sort of opacity with therapy or yoga or drugs, remedy that way of not knowing with good information and sound reason. The trouble is that everything we have seen tells us that wiping away opacity means also wiping away the other parts/steps/dimensions of experience; it means losing intimacy and urgency. —Maybe then it is a shadow, not as dark patch but as that which makes objects into objects, the impenetrability essential to their reality, the strange, ghostly background noise that lets them speak. —Right, maybe.

Here is the conundrum: opacity names that which exceeds my known capacities in an encounter with something that holds significance for me—exceeds my ways of describing, of understanding, and of knowing how to go on. It points to what is too much for me and what I want to rid myself of because it is a burden. But then I find I must also rid myself of what sets the encounter—and the thing— apart; I have lost the very thing, if a thing it is, that makes the encounter worth having. Once I expose it to the full blaze of concepts, it becomes flat and barren, not a mere shadow of itself, but itself a thing without a shadow.

Opacity is tied into intimacy and urgency like a knot we keep working to undo, not realizing, yet also somehow realizing, that without it those modes of being—those ways of hearing and speaking—would unravel. Another image, this knot, and likely not the last. In more abstract terms: opacity is the difficulty in the encounter with works of art and works of reflection, the difficulty of criticism.

THE DIFFICULTY OF CRITICISM

The difficulty of criticism—its opacity—is not something you come upon late in the game; it is there right from the start, in the encounter with the thing holding significance. Sometimes, though, it takes a while to notice what was there from the start. When I stood before my students and read aloud a passage from *The Trial* and, finding nothing to say about it, repeated it (with the same result), I felt I was facing not opacity nor some interesting shadow, but a very long seventy-five minutes. Only years later did I realize that my incapacity to speak that day was worth probing, which is how it was only halfway into writing this book that I discovered its beginning.

When I described my mishap many pages ago, I did not quote the passage that had me tied up in knots, not to protect a sore spot but because the particular words seemed of little consequence. Any passage from the novel, I thought, could have done just as well; in fact, any bit of writing, any gesture in paint or sound or flesh, could have given me the start. Quoting Kafka's words risked giving them too much weight, as though they, and they alone, held the key to my condition.

It is probably true that another passage could have served just as well, yet it is the sort of truth that is easy to declare and difficult to hold. Do I really believe that the lines that took my breath away are arbitrary? It is like thinking that *any* child could have taken the place of the children I have and could have been loved as intensely—no doubt true, but also impossible.

The truth is that the truth of the idea that any passage *could* have done was capable of taking root because on that day, with those students, in that mood, it was *this* passage and no other that got under my skin. Without the particularity of the instance, such a truth could not be universally acknowledged, not because, for lack of training in abstract thought, I require the use of "the baby walkers of judgment" (that's Kant scoffing at examples)[2] but because the truth of the phenomenon I am trying to describe—the way an encounter with a significant thing unfolds—flashes up only in *this* instance, and then *this* and *this* and *this*, a string of singulars that add up to no plural. Which is why the description must never lose sight of the singular, or risk losing its way.

Here is the passage, then. Josef K. is at his first interrogation. He is doing his best to sway the raucous crowd in his favor, enjoying the sound of indignation in his own voice, when a cry derails him:

> K. was interrupted by a shriek from the other end of the hall; he shaded his eyes so that he could see, for the dull daylight had turned the haze into a blinding glare. It was the washerwoman, whom K. had sensed as a major disturbance from the moment she entered. Whether or not she was at fault now was not apparent. K. saw only that a man had pulled her into a corner by the door and pressed her to himself. But she wasn't shrieking, it was the man; he had opened his mouth wide and was staring up toward the ceiling.[3]

What are you—what was I—supposed to say after this? That it is a good example of the alienation of Modern Man? (And of Modern Woman too, of course!) That it gives expression to the violence of this anonymous, bureaucratized world of ours? Or that this man shrieking and staring at the ceiling while pressing to his body the body of a woman, a washerwoman—that *this* image in *these* words—is too much?

This "too much," this surplus announcing itself as an insufficiency, is one way that opacity makes itself felt in encounters with the poetic. To get to know it better, I need to know where to find it. Is it in the thing I face? That is how we commonly speak: when I falter in trying to say something about Kafka's words, it is because *they* are too much— too weird, too good, too close to the bone. But it also makes sense to specify that these words are, at this moment, too much *for me*. Perhaps they are not too much for you; perhaps on another day, with other people, they are not even too much for me.

We are far enough into this book to know that quarreling about whether opacity in poetic criticism is a feature of the object (say, *The Trial*) or of the subject (say, me) is sure to get us off track. We have learned (if we didn't know already) that intimacy and urgency are not substances that are divisible between objects and subjects, nor are they features of these entities; they exist in between, or they do not exist. Because it is folded into intimacy and urgency, opacity too does not inhabit object or subject (wholly or in part) but is a mode of doing—a way of making—that runs athwart the two.

That accounts for why reflections on the peculiar power of poetic works so often center on ways of making. It need not trouble us that many of these reflections are preoccupied with what are commonly called "works of art"; the thinking they do applies to any form of poetic making, wherever it occurs.

THE STRANGE VOICE

If we turn to see how others in the Western tradition have written about the opacity we are trying to describe—the opacity in encounters with poetic works—we note right away how frequently the coming into being of the poetic is credited not to an author in sovereign possession of his craft and his wits, but to a stranger trespassing on this author, a stranger who remains in the shadows, nameless and mysterious. "Sing, O goddess, the anger of Achilles." "Tell me, O Muse, of that many-sided hero who traveled far and wide after he had sacked the famous town of Troy." So familiar are these opening words of the Homeric epics that we have learned not to stumble over the oddity of a poet setting out, not by establishing his own authority to tell a story, or even simply making known his wish to do so ("Let me tell you of that many-sided hero . . ."), but by calling on someone else to tell *him* the story. It surprises us not nearly enough that European literature opens not with one voice but two.

Both voices shape the coming into being of the poem. Both are present in it, yet not in the same way; it is not a duet that we witness. We hear just one voice, the poet's, but somehow altered, shifted out of its quotidian ways into a different register, and this shift is brought about by the second voice, inaudible yet urgent. What matters about this unearthly voice sounding "through" and "in" the poet is that it remains unassimilated. Even when the poet invites it in, it remains alien. No identity limits it, no knowledge or skill is ascribed to it, no trait specifies it—nothing other than the fact that it is and remains a stranger inhabiting the poet's voice.

We know at least one thing about this voice echoing in Homer's voice, do we not, namely that it is feminine. Does that fact not bring it down to earth and lift its veil of opacity, if only by a little? More likely the opposite: its femininity makes the voice not more familiar but less so. Many thinkers have shown that in Western conceptions (and not in these alone), any posited entity—subject, essence, voice, or the like—is shadowed by something from which it must be distinguished, some Other, and that the feminine serves as the most basic in a long line of others; the philosopher Simone de Beauvoir was among the first to say this. If anything, then, characterizing the voice as feminine foregrounds its utter alienness.

The stranger within, this intimate stranger, returns in Plato's account of how poetic works come into being. Socrates tells Ion, himself a singer of poetry, that the poet is "never able to compose until he has become inspired, and is beside himself, and reason is no longer in him. So long as he has this in his possession, no man is able to make poetry" (*Ion* 534b, in Lane Cooper's translation). The formula is plain: rather than possessing reason, the poet is possessed by unreason. Why resort to this artificial term, "unreason"? Why not say, as Socrates does, "enthusiasm" or "madness" or "Bacchic transport"? Because what possesses the poet remains, again, a blank and nothing more; there is no content here to madness or enthusiasm: no knowledge, no technique, no coherent experience, no positive marker. The content of transport is a form, the swerve marked by the *un-* in unreason, the perceptibly imperceptible shift in the voice of the poet. Power is wielded by what is missing, by the shadow cast by reason's withdrawal.

Socrates, too, names the muse as the source of this unreason—this blank in known ways of making—that invades the poet and therefore also poetry, but his commitment to the goddess is less than ironclad. What matters to him in this story—what matters also to us as we look to gain intimacy with opacity—is the logic of this blockage, not its precise location. Which is why the source of poetic power can shift, leaping from image to image, suddenly and capriciously. Try following Socrates as he leads up to the lines I quoted earlier:

> The lyric poets are not in their senses when they make these lovely lyric poems. No, when once they launch into harmony and rhythm, they are seized with the Bacchic transport, and are possessed. . . . For the poets tell us, don't they, that the melodies they bring us are gathered from rills that run with honey, out of glens and gardens of the Muses, and they bring them as the bees do honey, flying like the bees. And what they say is true, for a poet is a light and winged thing, and holy. . . . (534a–b)

We read the passage and reread it, but puzzlement will not lift. The lines zig and zag from image to image, and with every hairpin turn a new vista opens: the poets make lovely poems; they are seized by the madness of the maenads; they fly about like light and winged things; they collect poetry as bees collect honey; they are holy; they are beasts.

The point is not to have caught Plato in an inconsistency (assuming Socrates serves as Plato's mouthpiece here). The point, rather, is that it is manifestly of no consequence to him whether the right description of poets has them in the grip of the muse or buzzing with the bees, as long as it is understood—and this is crucial—that when they make poetry, they know not how they do. Plato has in mind singers of Homeric tales or of lyric songs, but his assessment holds for all poetic makers, no matter their material or the form their acts take. No skill or technique, no *techne* responsive to rational analysis and control, holds sway over their way of making, which is why it remains opaque— opaque to the poets themselves, opaque also to an observer as shrewd as Socrates. Poets do not make their products the way other human makers make theirs. Their way of making follows a different logic, a logic that amounts to eluding any known logic: perhaps it is divine, or perhaps it is beastly; perhaps it is holy or demonic or perhaps both. It may be more than human or less: the upshot is that it is not quite human. It has something *non*human about it. Which gives us another way of circumscribing opacity: the nonhuman lurking in the human being.

ARISTOTLE VERSUS PLATO

We found what we came looking for, an early, prestigious articulation of opacity that gives us a new way of speaking about it, a bonus we hadn't expected. We are ready to move on, yet something gives us pause. Perhaps what puts us on guard is the fickleness in Plato's tone when he speaks about poetry (here and elsewhere in his writings)— kind, even admiring one moment, ferocious the next. He must know that he is overstating his case, that many skills go into making a poem; he was a poet himself.

Knowing his other writings about poetry and poets, we come to suspect that the good cop in him finally works into the hands of the bad cop. It is not news that he has an axe to grind, an axe that he puts to ruthless use in the *Republic*: with the doggedness typical of zealots, he chips away at poetry until he has cut it clear off the body of his ideal polity. It is fair to ask, then: Why linger with a line of thinking that bears a murderous grudge against the very thing we wish to know better? And: if opacity flourishes in a habitat as toxic as this, is it wise to seek its closeness? Are there no alternatives?

There are; there always are. We could go to Aristotle's counter-programming in the *Poetics*, where the aim is to show that at bottom poetry is a *techne* like any other, like horsemanship, say, or statecraft. Its ways of making may seem convoluted, but with the right tools it can be disentangled, its ingredients enumerated, and its methods described in orderly fashion. There is much to learn from this book, not least the good news that Aristotle does not deem poets insane and their products worth banishing. But one thing he fails to do is to reach—even just reach *for*—that flare-up in the world that makes reality itself ecstatic, for the sake of which we go to poetic works—of art, of reflection, of any sphere, high, low, or middle. He steers clear of the scalding core of the matter, even when speaking of *Oedipus*, which is saying something. He gives us "fear" and "pity" and "catharsis" and some other terms with which to say useful things, but no language to describe, much less understand, how, faced with a poetic work, I might lose my bearings.

That is not a failing specific to Aristotle. The same is true of the countless efforts at regularizing and regulating (or, as philosophers now like to say, "naturalizing") poetry that arrive in his wake. In fact, from his and their point of view, this failure is no failure; it is a feature. The approach prides itself on sweeping away the cobwebs of mystification. And what is opacity but a mystification?

Taking this path does have its benefits. To begin, because the *Poetics* grants poetic making, and hence also poetry, the dignity of existing in the ambit of rationality, it has no need for an axe, and so no need for axe grinding. Instead, it can give itself over to a technical analysis of how poetry works, which is not something we can or wish to do without in criticism. Yet this approach has a chance of success only if poetry is reduceable to a principle that allows it to yield, and yield fully, to technical analysis.

For Aristotle, that principle is imitation, but it could take a different form; some evolutionary theorists, for example, like to think of all art as a signaling technique that aids sexual selection. Either way, the principle makes the poetic work responsive to analysis, leaving no remainder; *everything* in it turns out to be a form of imitation (or sexual signaling or whatever). Which makes sense: if art is technique all the way down, then technique must be responsible for every one of its significant features; that would distinguish a successful work, and failure would simply flag a violation of technique (or its absence—some part of a work may have been left blank). My task as critic would lie in sifting through the work for techniques, identifying them and assessing their aptness, and then adding it all up, coming to a judgment.

That is possible because, wearing Aristotelean glasses, I have no trouble recognizing a poetic work, for I always know, and know ahead of time, what it is *for*, just as knowing a wheel or a scouring pad depends on knowing their purposes. (Unless they fall into the hands of Marcel

Duchamp or Andy Warhol . . .) The work is now as transparent as the rational realm into which it has been absorbed: no stutter, no shadows, no opacity, no nonsense.

WHAT IN TECHNIQUE IS MORE THAN TECHNIQUE

The situation, then, takes roughly this form: in the one case, poetic making, held in the tight grip of the principle of imitation, is revealed to be *nothing but* craft, while in the other it involves *no* craft, so completely is it under the spell of inspiration. The two great philosophers, we now see, have thought themselves into opposite corners, where each can expound his theory at a safe distance from the other, yet— here is the downside—from where each fails to reach what is essential to the making of poetic works.

Where is it to be found, this essence of the poetic? Not somewhere in the middle: the work does not consist of fifty percent inspiration and fifty percent imitation, nor of some other ratio. What happens in the analysis of poetic works is not that we trace a chain of technical steps, one leading to the next, only suddenly to come upon a missing link, the point at which rational accounting runs aground, where, befuddled, we call in support from above. No, *every* feature of poetic making, and therefore every feature of a poetic work, issues from technique (where else?) and is therefore embedded in systems and histories of craft and of media, hence also responsive to social change, to shifts in political and material terms. Artworks—poetic things in general—are not cut off from the rest of the made world but are utterly part of it. Every work results from work; it is technique all the way down and all the way up.

At the same time, the work is also something more or, better yet, it is also something *else*: it is a technical device, yes, but with a difference. A device is technical if we can name (at least surmise) a purpose that bundles and coordinates the techniques acting upon it; otherwise, there is a jumble and no device. Encountering poetic works, I know I face no jumble but rather something that has the bearing of a device. It seems for all the world that a purpose is at work, yet I falter in naming it.

You feel that especially acutely when a work lays bare its technical makeup, like Christo's large wrapping installations. Reports about these often dwell on statistics: this many workers used this many miles of rope to secure this acreage of such and such a material around this well-known building or bridge—the sort of information one might deploy, in much the same form, to describe the building or bridge itself. And there *is* a sense in which the installation "imitates" the structure it envelops: it repeats the structure's shape, and in its composition is no less technical than the structure. It, too, is engineered.

Why, then, does the technical account of the poetic work feel paltry in a way that it does not when applied to a building or a bridge? I am reminded of projects that, having established that brain activity consists of nothing but battalions of synapses firing away, set out to account for the totality of mental life—longing, memory, regret, love—via fMRI imaging. Just because you know that everything is craft, or neural chemistry, or physics, does not mean that it is best described and best known in the language of technique or neurology or physics.

The reason the craft-based account fails is, again, because no principle of composition reveals itself. What is the purpose of Christo's work? Imitation? Sexual signaling? Social control? Diversion? Persuasion? One might offer: the thrill of seeing a well-known structure as though for the first time, and seeing it this way *because* it has been cloaked from view. Does that count as a purpose? Kant gives this mysterious phenomenon the equally mysterious title of "purposiveness without purpose" and identifies it as an indispensable feature of everything beautiful, but it can be extended to poetic works, beautiful or not, artistic or not. That is a way of saying that these works bring to the surface the ecstasy of reality. Which is a way of naming opacity: in their company I sometimes become so giddy that I do not know how to go on.

WHAT KIND OF THING IS THE POETIC THING?

The image of the two titans of ancient philosophy, each holding forth while trapped in a corner, opened some space for thinking, yet now, a few paragraphs on, we see that it might lead us astray, because the image itself is skewed. The problem is not that I have caricatured their thinking, which I have; a good caricature captures something essential about its subject and can deliver the truth with greater intensity than a scrupulous portrait. The problem is that the image suggests that the two inhabit corners of the same room. Do they? Do they put forward theories about the same thing?

Socrates, as we encounter him in Plato's *Ion* and *Phaedrus*, and Aristotle both claim to be speaking about "poetry," and though particulars differ—Socrates dwells mostly on Homeric tales and lyric songs, while the surviving sections of the *Poetics* deal with tragedy—we see enough kinship between them that without a second thought we pack them into the box labeled "poetry." Yet the gesture should give us pause: is "poetry" a box that holds poetic things?

The answer is yes if you are Aristotle. From that point of view, speaking about kinds of things makes sense: if there were no category of the poetic—if we didn't know what we mean when we talk about "drama" or "lyric" or "epic"—then the whole game would be up, for to unpack the craft needed to make something, you need to know what kind of a thing it is. Would you be able to speak about horsemanship or statecraft if you were unable to pick out horses or states? By this way of thinking, there is tragedy and dramedy, abstract painting and hiphop, yodeling and ambient music just as there are spoons and ceiling fans.

And in fact, this way of seizing "poetry" as though it were a defined body and then carving it up will do for most purposes. If you are running a bookstore, editing the literary section of a paper, or devising the departmental chart of a university, you tend to operate as an Aristotelean: your concept of poetry may be narrow (the way it mostly is today, extending no further than the lyric) or it may be broad enough to encompass all genres and subgenres of the verbal arts (perhaps even all arts, though that's pushing it). Either way, you know what kind of a thing "poetry" or a "piece of literature" is before having encountered it, even admitting borderline cases. (The concession in fact concedes very little; on the contrary, it shores up the taxonomy, for where would borderline cases be without borders to straddle?)

Yet if in my encounter with a thing I am not obtuse to what in that encounter may remain unknown or not quite known to me, if a thing or an act strikes me in a way that eludes the grasp of conceptions that I am able to deploy, if it delivers a charge of intensity that allows me—compels me—to lose my bearings and activates something that takes me beyond familiar ways of being and doing—if, in short, the thing or the act I encounter is *poetic*—then wielding the category of "poetry" is not just inapt: it gets in the way; it diminishes the encounter and deflects it into familiarity. It offers peace of mind just when I find myself unsettled.

This is where Plato, for all his hostility to the poetic, gives us access to a richer language to describe what slips through the fingers of concepts (accounting perhaps for the hostility). For in talking about poetry, he is not concerned with the genus or species of things, but rather with a thing that threatens to capsize the generic system—a thing, in other words, that is an act, a poetic act.

That may sound far-fetched, but in fact accords with every real encounter with the poetic. Which is why no bookshelf labeled "poetry," no news department, and no school can encompass all things poetic, for no definition will cleanly and enduringly separate literature from not-literature, sculpture from not-sculpture, dance from not-dance. Without a moment's notice, the one can issue into the other.

That does not mean that distinctions no longer matter. Few differences make themselves felt as flagrantly as the one between a poetic act and a nonpoetic act. But it does mean that poetic things—which are just poetic acts pressed into material—do not lend themselves to being corralled into categories with clear criteria of membership, categories like a literary canon, a museum collection, or a repertoire. Such categories do represent something real, often the force of power or of habit, but they are not reliable repositories for the poetic.

That is also why even the amplest understanding of "art" is at once too narrow and too broad to hold the poetic. Too narrow, because the poetic can flare up in any human situation: running my eyes over the rote prose of a news report, I come upon an arresting phrase, and all of a sudden the whole paper is on fire. Having a meal (sushi, for example), taking a walk, talking to friends, I may find that for some reason—because of an unexpected juxtaposition of textures, or the rise and fall of a voice, or the friction caused by adjacent images, or some other unnamable cause—my ways of taking in the world, of describing it, and of acting in it have shifted enough to make space for new possibilities, which may well arrive as new ways of being stymied. Yet the category of "art" is also too indiscriminate, for it can happen, and happens all the time, that even at the zenith of High Art—take the writings of Thomas Mann—the poetic drive gradually fizzles, leaving behind mostly prattle.

THE WORK OF ART VERSUS THE POETIC WORK

I am circling back to something I noted before, namely, that the term "poetic thing" can mislead no less than the term "work of art," for no thing is poetic from top to bottom. Calling it poetic does not mean that it has soaked up poetry in every pore.

That's obvious to anyone who has read a novel or sat through a dance performance, yet it is still difficult to keep in one's head; our habits of thought tend elsewhere. When offering an interpretation of a work of art, we critics feel compelled to discover "art" in every point of its objecthood, and if our account leaves blank spots, then that must be our failing. That is because in the prevailing conception of art *everything* in a work is meaningful, and meaningful not just in its own right but in relation to everything else in the work. Everything in it exists—and must exist—to give expression to the one meaning (even when it takes the form of the suspension of all determinable meanings).

The most arresting version of this conception of art that I know comes in the lectures on aesthetics that the philosopher Georg Wilhelm Friedrich Hegel gave at the University of Berlin in the 1830s. He thinks of art as a physical manifestation of "the true" (what I noncommittally called the "one meaning" that critics seek). The true inhabits the work of art the way the soul inhabits the human body, but even more fully and intensively: the true flashes up in *every* feature of the work, while the soul is scattered across the human body; each organ, Hegel says, "manifests . . . only some particular activity and partial emotion." Except the eye: the eye is the one organ in which "the whole soul appears as soul." Ears, nose, hands, toes—these manifest the soul, but only some aspect or other. By contrast, "in the eye the soul is concentrated and the soul does not merely see through it but is also seen in it." If we stay with the analogy and think of the work of art as a body, then it is a body that manifests the *whole* soul in *each* of its parts—a body consisting of nothing but eyes, "a thousand-eyed Argus," as Hegel says.[4]

Few of us have the cheek to put it this way, yet virtually all interpretations offered by us professionals go back to the Hegelian picture: the work of art means; it means everywhere; and everywhere it means the same thing. Even in its most trifling part, we can glimpse the work's soul.

This work of art, then, is unblemished by opacity, since its very idea entails utter transparency. The poetic work, on the other hand, is mired in opacity. It holds and releases intensifications unevenly. The intimacy it offers is fragile. Where the work of art is smooth, the poetic work is lumpy. As for its structure and development, there is no place where its parts gather into a final form (no teleology governs it), not because as the product of human beings perfection remains out of reach, but because the work invites participation and continuation. In that way, it is essentially incomplete or, as Friedrich Schlegel says: it is fragmentary. It does not come to rest in a settled form but keeps working, which is what makes it a *work*: a work is a work as long as it works. Even when I ardently wish it to stay as it is, I know it could have taken a different shape. And in fact, at different times and in different contexts, it *does* take a different shape.

What am I getting at? Not that artistic works and poetic works inhabit discrete domains. The poetic, I have said, can discharge its force anywhere, and works of art are not exempt; they may even turn out to offer especially promising staging grounds for the poetic. If now we imagine a Venn diagram, where the gray overlapping area holds objects that check off the boxes of both "art" and "poetry," we would still be misapprehending things. Rather than naming classes of objects, the terms alert us to different forms of comportment. What Hegel and the tradition after him have taught us to call a "work of art" is the sort of thing I carefully pick up and examine, assured that from every angle I will see the same deep thing, though also aware that "seeing" is far from a simple act and requires training and practice. But once I know how to divine the meaning, I know I will encounter it every time I look, for the work of art is the sort of thing that remains unchanged. It rests contently in its self-sameness, indifferent to my attention.

The poetic work works differently. Indifference is not its thing. It seduces me, plays with me, manipulates me, requires things of me (attention, interest, engagement, laughter, curiosity, . . .). It calls on me to do something—with it, with myself, with you.

This doing entails understanding, which is, again, why interpretation and making are not mutually exclusive ways of acting. Like the artwork, the poetic work moves in relation to meaning, yet rather than holding and possessing meanings outright, it flirts with them as it flirts with me. Its significance (distinct from its fixed meaning) comes into play—*is* in play—to the degree that it matters to me. Sitting on a shelf or hanging on a wall, a work continues to be artfully constructed, yet it is not poetic—not yet. It *becomes* poetic once it activates something in me.

And my activation—I have said it—does not result from a message enjoining me to become active, a message passed from A to B, from the object to me. A poetic work does not communicate its poetry through propositions in need of decoding; a poem, "though it is composed in the language of communication, is not used in the language-game of communication."[5] That is Wittgenstein's way of describing the opacity in the way the poetic work unfolds its force. What makes the work poetic, what can make *me* poetic, is that the words and images and sounds it marshals somehow overflow the normal channels of symbolic communication.

What, then, happens when I look the poetic work in the eyes? Do I glimpse "the true" of which Hegel speaks? It depends. If the true is assumed to take the form of a philosophical proposition, then the most flagrant encounters with the poetic may lead me to miss it. But if the true can erupt in an obscure fierceness that unmoors me, then yes: in my encounter, I am led to acknowledge the true.

THE EYE OF THE WORK, THE EYE OF THE BEHOLDER

The fact that the poetic flashes up unpredictably and erratically has to do with me as much as it does with the work. In one reading of *Madame Bovary*, the scene of Emma gagging at the basket of fragrant apricots that her husband presses on her, the same basket that had delivered a note from her lover ending their affair, strikes me as so beautiful and cruel that I put down the book, and had you been there, I would have wished to tell you about it. Yet reading it again years later, I glide right past the passage. Has it become less poetic? To my eyes and ears, that evening, in that mood—yes. I may have been distracted, and things may turn out otherwise next time we meet. They might be different for you, which, depending on our relationship, may make a difference to me.

Now it sounds as though the object and its composition no longer matter and the poetic finally is in the eyes and ears and moods of the beholder. Is it? Sometimes it can seem so. It can happen that someone sees real beauty in a pile of things that have been dumped on the roadside. There are people with an eye for such epiphanies of beauty or of sadness or of humor. Do the sparks of poetic energy shimmer only in their eyes? We who may be insensible to the flare-up of the poetic in the everyday may be inclined to say yes, but it likely does not seem that way to them. What arrests their attention is the world itself; it is the arrangement of tossed objects that is beautiful or aching, not a way of seeing nor some attitude.

And when we are not theorizing, we credit that account. We acknowledge that in the company of some people the ordinary world is no longer ordinary. Not that it looks or appears that way: it actually *is* extraordinary. It is what we say about the worlds of Agnès Varda or Abbas Kiarostami or Werner Herzog. People who see poetry in a pile of debris make the world into a more interesting place, which is a way of saying: they *make* the world—make it poetically by virtue of attending to it, framing some segment of it, bringing to light a constellation hidden in it. They are poets of the given.

Even in this extreme case of "found poetry," then, we would hesitate to locate the poetic work in the eye of the percipient alone. But most of the time, encounters with the poetic do not take this form. Most of the time, I do not blunder into the ecstasy or the difficulty of reality (by which, again, is meant the way its beauty or its cruelty—its intensity—can be too much to bear) without preparation or context, without a history. In trying to describe what remains opaque in the encounter with poetic works, I have emphasized the ways in which these encounters unseat what can be known through Aristotelean technical examination. Yet I have not said often enough that without technique there would be nothing to unseat. That is not just logical cleverness (in the sense that undoing X implies the prior existence of X) but gets at the phenomenology of the encounter with something that bowls me over: unseating the technical account, or any account established through conventions of knowledge, itself demands conduct shaped by technique and knowledge. It demands education. (Not that *Bildung* will always get you there; as often as not, it deflects you.)

Which prompts me to repeat what I've said before, repeat it because it is an idea easy to acknowledge and difficult to retain: that poetic criticism is not a kind of criticism, but can come into being, and can also vanish, in anything we care to label criticism. No bit of philology is turgid enough, no critique of ideology hectoring enough not to allow—somewhere—flashes of the poetic. Even where the author does his best to hide behind shopworn phrases, the writing can suddenly make room for a phrase whose unforeseen turn shakes me from my slumber, or can fall into a helpless stammer that testifies, perhaps, to an upheaval of experience. The poetic is dormant in every act of criticism, as it is in every human act; the question is just whether it is permitted to stir to life.

HOW TO LEAP OVER ONE'S OWN SHADOW

What looked at first like a symmetrical difference between Plato's account and Aristotle's turns out to be lopsided, something I should have seen right away. The one affirms ways of knowing how—how to make a work of art and how to respond to it—while the other insists that there is no knowing how a poetic work comes into being and therefore no knowing how to speak about it coherently. Know-how and don't-know-how are not two parallel ways of doing: one is a way, the other a nonway—an impasse, a wormhole in experience, a trip (delirious, hallucinatory), a stumble.

This chapter began with the idea that opacity consists of a blockage in knowing how—put crudely, that it belongs in the "Platonic" corner, with inspiration, Bacchic transport, dark unreason, and the rest. But now it seems that opacity in fact names, *also* names, not one "side" or the other, but the lopsidedness between knowing and not knowing how to respond to a poetic act. What remains obscure in my encounters with the poetic—that is, in criticism—is the precise entanglement of technical explication and passionate engagement. The poetic act is fully technical, and so poetic criticism is fully technical, yet it is also other than technical. And I never know when in an encounter a change in energy will take it from the one side to the other.

Opacity as a shift, then, a swerve in known ways of doing. The swerve is a formal swerve, true, but it is not purely formal. It tends to take the shape of an obstruction, a grinding in the gears of action, a stammer in speech, an abrasion left by familiar forms. That does not mean that opacity must arrive with a negative affective load; sometimes the stutter is triggered by joy or bemusement. But it does appear first as a negation (of ways of perceiving, knowing, speaking, acting), a limitation of what is given, though we know, even if we forget, that its value changes: the limitation can become the springboard for breaching the limits of established ways.

This ebb and flow—how loss converts, unaccountably, into a plenitude of new possibilities—often characterizes writings that describe what I have been calling opacity, or something close enough. "No poet, no artist of any art, has his complete meaning alone," T. S. Eliot remarks.[6] Reading this, all our attention is focused on the deficit of meaning the poet suffers. That, we think, is where the poet remains opaque to her or his own meaning; insufficiency, we think, is another name for opacity. Which, again, is not wrong. But what makes it right, what gives a rounder, deeper sense of opacity's potential, is remembering that it is this lack that ignites the unimaginably vast power that Eliot sees in the work, a power to alter "all the works of art which preceded it"—*all*. That, to Eliot, is what it means to stand in a tradition: rather than being bound by the old, "the new (the really new) work" modifies every one of the "existing monuments" that came before it, rearranging them, all of them, into a newly meaningful configuration (15). The poet's fragmented meaning transmutes itself into the wholeness of meaning that only the tradition offers. That is not how I might put it, but no matter; what is compelling is the logic of opacity that Eliot discovers: out of utter incompletion emerges utter completion: ebb, flow.

Another example. When the poet-philosopher Gaston Bachelard writes that "in poetry, non-knowing is a primal condition," we feel confirmed in our guiding intuition that at the heart of poetry there is a blankness (and confirmed, too, by Bachelard finding it not in the person of the poet, as Eliot does, but in poetry itself).[7] But that is not the end of it, for this obscure heart of poetry, blank though it is, pulsates. Despite the prefix of negation, the non-knowing of which Bachelard speaks names not the suspension or retraction of skill or understanding or consciousness. It is, rather, a reservoir of potentiality, of potency. "Non-knowing is not a form of ignorance but a difficult transcendence of knowledge," Bachelard notes, quoting the words of the poet-essayist Jean Lescure, though one feels him wishing he had written them himself. A philosopher of life, Bachelard is drawn to the language of vivacity: the non-knowing in poetry, he writes, promotes "an increase of life, a sort of competition of surprises that stimulates our consciousness and keeps it from becoming somnolent" (17).

That is well put, though it risks underplaying things, for more is at work here than keeping the mind from nodding off. A thing, an act, an encounter leaves me drained of words and disoriented because it surpasses what I am capable of holding; yet if I find a way of turning this surplus intensity into an act—*if*—then I wake up to new way of doing and making. Which is why the non-knowing in poetry is not the absence of knowledge but its "transcendence": I do things that I did not know I knew how to do, surprising myself at how I take part in stretching the limits of spontaneity, take part because the stretch is no achievement of my willful doing alone.

"No poet . . . has his complete meaning alone." "In poetry, non-knowing is a primal condition." Once we learn to hear in such negations the affirmation of the yin-yang movement of opacity—how its power to veil is its power to disclose ways of seeing and hearing, ways of knowing and acting—we recognize their kinship to utterances that have struck us mainly by their inscrutability. "My pictures are wiser than me," the painter Gerhard Richter has said in an interview.[8] That sounds like either the logic is false or the modesty, but we now see that it offers a good description of poetic making. When the thing I have made looks back at me, I see neither an expression of the feelings and thoughts with which I maintain an everyday closeness (my "inner life") nor a testament to my social embeddedness (my "identity") but something strangely familiar brought into being by a familiar stranger. It can be a pleasure, a thrill, to come face to face with something made by someone who coincides with me while differing from me: shrewder than I know myself to be, more honest, less weak—wiser.

How to reach that form of making? How to become that familiar stranger? In the same interview, Richter says: "I have to use some strategy . . . to be able to leap over my own shadow." To leap over own's own shadow—what a weird and wonderful image (an idiom in German). If I pull off the warped acrobatics it describes, I land beside and beyond myself. It's a cheerful way of picturing the logic behind Bachelard–Lescure's forbidding talk of a "transcendence of knowledge." You don't need an advanced degree in philosophy to get it.

Now we see Aristotelean eyebrows being raised. Does such a logic-defying leap not vault Richter, and us, into the territory of unreason, of possession and frenzied transport? Is opacity, rather than dwelling in interesting obscurity, not just obscurantist? Perhaps; perhaps there is no way of talking about opacity without risking what some will call mystification. But note that Richter speaks of using "some strategy" to find a way of leaping over his own shadow. A strategy: pacing the studio waiting to be teleported into the company of the maenads does not count as a strategy, nor does passing a brush aimlessly over the canvas until the right design turns up. Richter is a painter. A painter paints, wipes clear, makes sketches, mixes paint and remixes it, repaints; sometimes, he starts over. Whatever the strategy, it happens in painting. It is embedded in the craft of painting and in its history.

Seen from this end, the image of the leap seems mistaken or at least misleading, for only in rare cases does a fully fledged shape—the right line or color, the right pause in an onstage dialogue, the right metaphor or line of thought, let alone the right tone or mood—present itself in one fell swoop. Usually, makers fuss over their material: they combine, erase, substitute, turn upside down, test, undo, redo, re-undo—a process so completely immersed in technique that it can seem to them that what matters is not some grand idea but just getting the material into the right shape, here, in this remote corner of the thing being made: *this* patch, *this* gesture, *this* word. At some point they pause and step back. They may find themselves right where they started, but then again, they may find that unbeknownst to themselves they have somersaulted over their own shadows. What looks back at them, they note with a mixture of bewilderment and bliss, is more intelligent and wiser than they are.

The iterative process of revision is how the added share of wisdom or joy or wit can make its way into the painting or writing or dancing. The writer George Saunders describes it well:

> Revising by the method described is a form of increasing the ambient intelligence of a piece of writing. This, in turn, communicates a sense of respect for your reader. As text is revised, it becomes more specific and embodied in the particular. It becomes more sane. It becomes less hyperbolic, sentimental, and misleading. It loses its ability to create a propagandistic fog. Falsehoods get squeezed out of it, lazy assertions stand up, naked and blushing, and rush out of the room. . . .
> This mode of revision . . . is ultimately about imagining that your

reader is as humane, bright, witty, experienced and well intentioned as you, and that, to communicate intimately with her, you have to maintain the state, through revision, of generously imagining her. You revise your reader up, in your imagination, with every pass. You keep saying to yourself: "No, she's smarter than that. Don't dishonour her with that lazy prose or that easy notion."

And in revising your reader up, you revise yourself up too.[9]

That is a superb description of how books and pictures come to be wiser than their makers. Which also accounts for why it is often so disappointing to meet writers (painters, . . .) of works you admire and love: having rallied their skills to revise themselves up, once the work is done, they are left with nothing to hold on to and drop back down into their everyday selves.

All of this makes the leap over one's shadow seem less flamboyant than we first imagined. It is not clear that it even qualifies as a leap. It may just be an imperceptibly small step, taken somewhere along the way, during any of the innumerable tweaks imposed on the material. Did I leap over my shadow when I added some blue where it had no business being? Or when I cut the fancy adjective that I had been so pleased to find after rummaging through the thesaurus for twenty minutes? It is also possible that what Richter calls the leap is not one of the many tiny steps but their sum. Perhaps it presents itself as a leap only after the fact or to someone not involved in the process of making (that is, to the rest of us).

WHY NON-KNOWING IS THE PRIMAL CONDITION OF POETRY

Right about now we may think that the process, broken down into iterative steps, has finally been demystified and that talk of leaping, and of opacity, has been revealed to be a muddle. In fact, the opposite is true. The process remains as enigmatic as ever. Even Saunders, a trained engineer partial to no-nonsense explanation, concedes—no, just *says*: "An artist works outside the realm of strict logic." Frightened by the boldness of his own assertion, he rushes to call on the higher authority of Donald Barthelme: "The writer is that person who, embarking upon her task, does not know what to do," which by now has a familiar ring for us. It is a version of what the critic and scholar Barbara Johnson liked to say in conversation: "When I write, I follow my unconscious." (You knew not to ask: But how? Also not: What kind of unconscious do you possess—or does it possess you?—that your prose ends up so lucid?) I take her to be saying, roughly, that she looks for some strategy to leap over her own shadow.

Richter's phrase takes the two models of poetic making, the technical (strategy) and the inspirational (leap), and yokes them together, even though officially they are not on speaking terms, not to make peace, but because poetic making needs them to be entangled. No leap without strategy, but also no strategy without a shadow; the strategy can only be "*some* strategy," as Richter says, never *this* strategy. Inspiration is embedded in technique, yes, but it is not exhausted by it. Who knows how you get to the point of leaping over your own shadow—certainly not by following the straight and narrow path of a method.

This tends to come as dismaying news to students who want to know what they must do to earn an A when writing an essay, which is understandable. But opacity cannot be solved like an algebraic equation. Unlike the dark side of the moon, it does not relinquish its mystery when confronted with enough ingenuity, for it is not—let's say it once more—a region of obscurity to be tamed with good lighting, but rather a way in which knowing-how surpasses itself. It is why non-knowing remains the primal condition of poetic making.

GENIUS

There is another question that has been nagging me: can it be that all this time, without admitting or even realizing it, I have been talking about genius? If so, should that trouble me? It does make me uneasy to be seen with a figure that is so unabashedly theatrical. When it makes its entrance in the aesthetic theories of the eighteenth and nineteenth centuries, it is inevitably to a drum roll. Many who have written about genius, promoters and detractors alike, see in it a figure standing aloof from techniques of making—a figure, in fact, *designed* to stand aloof from craft, from know-how, from labor. If we followed this line of thinking, then before long we would find ourselves in the thick of mystification: since, in this understanding, genius bears no resemblance—none—to any form of making we know, we would be asked to recognize a form of making defined by the fact that we *fail* to recognize it. You see the problem.

But there is another way of thinking of genius, one suggested by Immanuel Kant. Here genius signifies a way of using technical means to make something that outstrips what could be made by technical means. Does that sound like a paradox? No more than the striking phrase by John Williams that we came across pages ago, namely, that literature opens a way of "knowing something through words that could not be put in words."[10] The paradox is shorthand, like the image of the leap over one's shadow.

And longhand? For Kant, genius is the solution to an incongruity in the making of art. Actually, the incongruity remains insoluble, and genius does no more than name that fact. We have come to know this incongruity well: works are made using techniques—their structure is not arbitrary—but the precise makeup of these techniques remains strangely out of reach. That is not because they are shut away in the artist's head (or wherever artists store their know-how). Asking the artist, looking at letters and diaries, does not help, for the artist is as clueless as we are. "The author of a product that he owes to his genius does not know himself how the ideas for it come to him," Kant explains in the *Critique of Judgment*, "and also does not have it in his power to think up such things at will or according to plan."[11] The author does not know, because the coming into being of art withdraws from knowledge, at least knowledge bounded by concepts. If we had complete knowledge of the techniques that brought into being the work of art, then we would know the work completely. We could hold it up to a standard governing those techniques, compare the two, and judge the quality of the work, the way we do with any ordinary useful thing. But works of art, says Kant, are the sort of things that refuse to be judged in such a way: knowing the ingredients that go into a tragedy does not give you the tools to come to a judgment about *Oedipus* or *Lear*.

What is the role of genius, then? It "give[s] the rule to art" and at the same time throws a veil over that rule, making it inaccessible (307). It pulls the work into the orbit of human making (for human beings make things not by instinct but by following rule-governed techniques) and, at once, shields it from human intelligence. Put another way: it names the way the artist's knowledge of his own work comes with a blind spot, names an opacity in the artist's self-knowledge, the place where the artist remains a stranger to himself. But genius is not a psychological condition; it does not diagnose an anomaly in the person of the artist. It describes, rather, something in the logic—the grammar, the structure—of experience, namely, the opacity that prevails whenever I face something whose significance I cannot quite bear. It is true that to a philosopher such as Gilles Deleuze the concept of genius is anathema, but listen to what he has to say about the great writer:

> A great writer is always like a foreigner in the language in which he expresses himself; even if this is his native tongue. At the limit, he draws his strength from a mute and unknown minority that belongs only to him. He is a foreigner in his own language: he does not mix another language with his own language, he carves out a nonpreexistent foreign language within his own language. He makes the language itself scream, stutter, stammer, or murmur.[12]

Does this foreign language within one's own language not describe the phenomenon of hitting upon just the technique that outstrips known techniques?

Another thing to retain from Kant's meditation on genius: he does not oppose it to concepts nor to thinking. His genius is not a cauldron of irrationality, divine or demonic, from which the artist draws inspiration. It is rather, as Kant writes elsewhere, "originality in thinking."[13] It belongs to thinking—the originality is *in* thinking— yet exceeds it, since what is truly new in thinking cannot be fully accounted for by thinking itself. It is the nameless fever that sometimes grips thinking and pushes it beyond itself, a fever incurable by more or better thinking—by self-examination, psychological research, or therapy. If the unconscious is not the negation of consciousness but a glitch within it, then a good term for genius—but also for opacity— would be unthinking: a shadow in thinking that yields a surfeit of thinking.

This is what we have, then: genius partakes of craft and know-how and labor, hence of rationality and thinking, and fully so; it does not hide in an unexplained leftover, nor is it a magic potion with which to spike regular, everyday technique. Like every other instance of human making, it is technical all the way up and down. But: techniques can be combined, developed, and deployed in endless iterations. It can happen that thanks to "some strategy" they find themselves torqued into a configuration that speaks to me in a new language. Which is the point at which we say that the poet works outside the realm of strict logic.

This intensified technique—in a painting by Richter, say—solicits a different comportment from me: it asks me to look differently, to listen, to take pleasure, to wonder, perhaps also to do something—speak to you, write, make something—all in ways that differ from my quotidian ways, if only by a bit. It activates something in the material and in the techniques shaping the material, which in turn activates something in me, inciting an intensification in my own engagement with what surrounds me, an engagement that may materially differ from what I encountered (seeing the painting may, for example, lead to an intensification of words).

In poetic making (I have said), know-how and don't-know-how are joined in an enigmatic, twisted knot, which might as well bear the title of genius. Genius is the name—an overworked name but still—for a way of making in which technique goes beyond itself, a name for the mystery in plain sight of poetic making.

Another approximation to opacity, then: the mystery in plain sight of poetic making. Genius is not opaque because its form of making has been withdrawn from view (unlike the craftsman's production, we might suppose, which takes place in the open workshop, on the street or on YouTube, before our eyes). It is opaque precisely because nothing is hidden. The documentary about Gerhard Richter, from which I have quoted, for long minutes shows him at work: he climbs a ladder holding a brush attached to a long stick; he applies a stripe of red paint to an enormous canvas; he then gets down from the ladder and considers the canvas from a distance—actions we might see performed by any first-year studio arts student. Yet sometimes out of the ordinary the extraordinary emerges, not by sleight of hand, but by injecting common techniques with urgency.

What the leap over one's own shadow signifies, what opacity in making anything poetic (criticism included) names, is the obscurity in technique itself, the obscurity of knowing when to add, when to subtract, when to keep going and when to start over, when to stop. Which is why Bachelard-Lescure calls the transcendence of knowledge "difficult." Try leaping over your shadow.

CRITICISM IS MAKING

Eliot, Bachelard, Richter, Saunders, Kant—they all aim to account for the mystery in poetic making. Does that help us get closer to poetic criticism, something we have been trying to do all book long? Not on the face of it. Like many thinkers of his time, Kant takes genius to be a feature of the artist, not of the critic. The incomplete meaning, the non-knowing, the leaping over shadows that our witnesses talk about apply to the poet or the painter; nobody says anything about a critic. This is in keeping with what aesthetic and poetic theories teach, namely, that "production" and "reception" are not just distinct, but polar activities: at the extremes, the one is imagined as pure productivity, expending without recompense (like God or Nature), while the other is pure receptivity, absorbing the output of the first pole.

This picture continues to orient our own ideas about the roles of "artist" and "critic." If anything, we have deepened the division. We imagine the main tasks of the critic—understanding, evaluation, judgment—not only as bereft of the maker's creativity but as hostile to creativity, as destructive: we analyze the work to take it apart; we "undermine" its supposed pretensions; we deconstruct, and with relish. So gleefully do we take the hammer to the work that someone like the poet-critic Eve Sedgwick feels obliged to call on us to pull ourselves together and do some reparative work for a change.[14]

One could counter the bipolar picture by calling on other witnesses, on Friedrich Schlegel (who coined the concept of "poetic criticism"), on Emerson ("One must be an inventor to read well," he would testify), on Walter Benjamin (whose true critic "forgets to pass judgment"), or on Stanley Cavell, who has written: "Describing one's experience of art is itself a form of art; the burden of describing it is like the burden of producing it."[15] (Under cross-examination, it would become clear that the "art" of which Cavell speaks names neither craft, as in "the art of French cooking," nor the spiritualized art of Hegel's philosophy, but a close kin to what I have been calling poetic making.) But that would likely not persuade anyone for whom the difference between production and reception is primary. It is true that criticism is not "the same thing" as art: painting a painting is not the same thing as writing about a painting. That is obvious. It is also trivial. Criticism is not the same thing as innumerable other things, and neither are singing and painting and candlestick making. Who would doubt that different genres exist, each rooted in distinct materials and techniques, each with its own history, each occupying its own place in society?

I have not been seeking to describe the genre of criticism, nor its social and historical place. My aim rather has been to find how criticism can become poetic—or, in keeping with the idea of looking for poetry in the adverb: how criticism can be done *poetically*. This adverbial shift follows the same mysterious path wherever it is encountered—in writing, in painting, in mathematics, in criticism, in politics, in philosophy, in all domains of human making.

THE POET OF THE POET

If in trying to learn about poetic making I have been drawn to reflections on art and aesthetics, it is because thinkers have traditionally located that form of making in the domain of art. That is a mistake, one that can lead us to miss the flare-up of the poetic elsewhere, in criticism for example. But in seeking to remedy it, another mistake lies in wait, this the flip side of the first. In this picture, the critic, previously starved of all creative juices, is now submerged by them. Not enough that he is imagined to be the artist's equal; he must top the artist at his, the artist's, own game. "The true reader," the poet Novalis offers, "must be the enlarged author."[16] It is easy to fail to notice how extravagant the claim is that these simple words make: the true reader is not a reader, as you and I may have thought, but an author, and not just *an* author but *the* author: the reader is the author of the work. In fact, he is more than the author. He is—he "must be"—"the enlarged author," a vaster version of this already vast agency: all that the author is and then some. "The true translator," Novalis writes elsewhere and means the true interpreter and true critic, "must be the poet of the poet."[17] No longer the antipoet, the critic is now the poet squared.

Novalis's friend and collaborator Friedrich Schlegel, too, gestures in this direction. When facing poetic works, Schlegel writes, it is "essential" that one "complete them and in part carry them out within oneself."[18] An extraordinary thought: the critic must complete the work. The word translates *ergänzen*, literally "to make whole." Why is it "essential" to complete the work? Because it belongs to the essence of modern poetic works to come into the world incomplete. "Many of the works of the ancients have become fragments. Many modern works are fragments as soon as they are written."[19] That includes this very declaration, which, like the passage I quoted earlier, was published by Schlegel under the heading "Fragments."

The pull of the idea of fragment and whole, of incompletion demanding completion, is prodigious. Even Walter Benjamin, a poetic critic if ever there was one, cannot withstand it. In a dissertation on the concept of criticism in German Romanticism, he sets out to show "that the Romantics called for poetic criticism," which he glosses as "suspending the difference between criticism and poetry."[20] What does that entail? Here is one summation Benjamin gives:

> Criticism is not meant to do anything other than discover the secret tendencies of the work itself, fulfill its hidden intentions. It belongs to the meaning of the work itself—that is, in its reflection that the criticism should go beyond the work and make it absolute. This much is clear: for the Romantics, criticism is far less the judgment of a work than the method of its conclusion.[21]

He concludes the passage with the phrase we just quoted: "It is in this sense that the Romantics called for poetic criticism, suspending the difference between criticism and poetry." Is it? Is it "*in this sense* that the Romantics called for poetic criticism"? That promises too much and delivers too little. Promises too much by promoting the critic to the position of the author's literary executor: criticism is to "discover the secret tendencies of the work," to "fulfill its hidden intentions," to "make it absolute"—in short: to serve as "the method of its conclusion." Yet that amounts precisely *not* to "suspending the difference between criticism and poetry," rather charging criticism with a power of which poetry itself is bereft: the power to reveal and to realize all intentions, to become absolute, to conclude. It is just in the *lack* of this power—and opacity is nothing but this lack—where the generative power of poetry lies, hence also where the power of poetic criticism lies. It is a lack—and a power—that Benjamin denies the critic.

If criticism is to be poetic, then the opacity in the poetic work—the way it remains insufficient to itself—must also remain a core feature of criticism. If "no poet . . . has his complete meaning alone" (to recall

Eliot's diagnosis), that goes for the "poet of the poet" too. Benjamin makes it sound as though two incompletions join to form a completion. But I do not set out with a hole in myself and then seek something—an artwork, say—that might plug it, nor do I spot a lack in a work that I then rush to fill. It is not up to me to mend a fragment nor to make amends for it.

FALLING

We are spiraling back to a point we reached in earlier pages: I open myself to intimacy with a work not by setting out to establish mastery over it (by discovering its secrets, fulfilling its hidden intentions, making it absolute, becoming *the* author). How then? By letting it impose itself on me? Surrendering to a work might be a first step, but it certainly cannot also be the last, for to do criticism poetically, I must act on my own account. So I must allow the work to act on me in a way that unleashes my own springs.

How might this work? Consider how certain paintings ask of the viewer to take a certain stance, a certain *di*stance, and a certain relation to light. I can of course decide to stand inches from the canvas, but in that case I see brushstrokes, not the painting. Or I can gaze at it from the far end of the hall and from there recognize a vague arrangement of shapes and colors. Part of what I do in a gallery, as I move about, eyes fixed on a painting, is to find out where *it* wants me to stand. Sometimes I find it right away; at other times it takes several approaches; and then there are times when the spot eludes me, for which I often blame the painting.

"Presenting anew what has been presented" (Schlegel); looking to become the "enlarged author" (Novalis); seeking to "carry out" the work in myself (Schlegel again)—these are ways of naming the search for a place from which the work calls to be read by me. Criticism involves, above all, not a way of uncovering a hidden meaning in an object but, rather, a process in which I experience something that exceeds my own capacities.

Rather than naming a momentary ecstasy, becoming vulnerable names a process involving a potentially enduring change, one whose exact outlines may remain obscure to me for a while, perhaps forever.

The true force of a reading, the most profound way in which it occasions a change in my world, is often not transparent to myself.

This offers us another go at understanding the scene with which I opened this book, holding Kafka's novel in my hands and not knowing what to say about it: I was seeking, and failing, to find the point from which the novel wishes to be read. The text spoke to me, but in ways that surpassed me. It touched me, but I could not grasp it. It knew something about me that I didn't. My stutter was vivid acknowledgment of my opacity to myself.

This line of thinking is congenial to the enigmatic psychoanalytic insight that when I read, my unconscious reads. I understand that to be a way of saying that, in reading, a certain relation to the world is activated in me, a relation that can never remain fully under my sway and whose shape emerges only belatedly.[22] If we take this idea seriously, then we no longer feel the need to say: *this* is what this passage mean: *this* thought, constellation, idea—thus far hidden—is really what it is about. Rather, we are more inclined to say: I see what sort of world I find myself in; I know where to stand and what to do next. Or else, when reading something by, say, Kafka, we might say: I don't know what it wants from me; I don't know how to go on.

Facing poetic works from a place of vulnerability requires, then, a certain surrender, a passivity unknown and anathema to scholarly criticism. How to imagine this passivity? As it happens, Kafka himself dwelled on the question. In January 1904, twenty years old, he writes in a letter to his childhood friend Oskar Pollak:

> I think we ought to read only the kind of books that bite and stab us. If the book we're reading doesn't wake us up with a blow on the skull, what are we reading it for? So that it will make us happy, as you write? Good Lord, we'd be just as happy if we had no books, and the kind of books that make us happy, we could, in a pinch, write ourselves. But we need the books that affect us like a misfortune that pains us deeply, like the death of someone we loved more than ourselves, like being banished to the woods far from everyone, like a suicide. A book must be the axe for the frozen sea within us.[23]

The passage is quoted a lot; you find it all over the internet. Still, every time I come across it, it takes my breath away. It delivers the kind of body blow that it itself craves.

But having the breath knocked out of you can render you insensible to muted features of the world. The flagrancy of the images that Kafka hurls at us (or rather at poor Oskar), the very flagrancy that makes them so hard to forget, can intimidate a reader into crediting the passage with a greater truth than it, in fact, discloses. After learning that the only kind of book worth its salt is one that slices through your soul, do you dare take a stand for gentler encounters?

The scene does capture something real, but this real occupies no more than a narrow band on the very edge of the kind of vulnerability I have been seeking to describe. It is possible that a book might affect a reader "like the death of someone we loved more than ourselves," though I cannot claim to have felt that myself. But a book might also affect readers in many other, less extravagant ways that still bring about a change in thoughts and minds and lives.

Kafka's account is so strong that it bends the relationship between book and reader out of shape. All agency, all force, all meaning is wielded by the book, while the reader stands exposed, passive and suffering, victim of a mighty writing machine. But losing our bearings while we read is mostly not, I think, a matter of being seized against our will by an alien force. If we are struck by a textual bolt, it is not because it arrives out of the blue. If the book bites and stabs us, it is not because it has caught us wholly unawares.

How then? If the experience in my encounter with poetic works does not occur against my will, have I then somehow willed it? Is it right to say I "seek" the book that wounds me? I do not seek it the way someone going to a horror movie seeks the thrill of being terrified, for I do not reach for an experience with a familiar outline. Yet it is also not simply visited upon me. How to describe this intermediate zone in which I am neither fully passive nor fully active, the zone in which the vulnerability born of intimacy unleashes an urgency of being and doing?

The philosopher Maurice Merleau-Ponty offers an analogy apropos of a different phenomenon. What happens, he asks, when I "try" to fall asleep? I am not usually felled by sleep against my volition, nor can I will its arrival, as I can attest when insomnia grips me. Instead, I get myself into a position where I may receive sleep. True, I do not put myself to sleep, but rather *fall* asleep, which registers the loss of willing. Yet I do not usually fall asleep the way a brick falls to the ground;

rather, I allow myself to fall, I get myself in the right place for this falling to happen to me.

This getting-into-position is itself not something that just happens to me but is something I must learn. It takes years of practice—of clutching the right objects and drifting into the right kinds of reveries—to learn to do something as seemingly simple and natural as falling asleep. Some of us, perhaps most of us, never master it, and even when we think we have, we find it slipping away the moment the night demons rear their heads.[24]

What is the point of the story? Not that my encounters with poetic works lull me to sleep. On the contrary, they stir me from my slumber, and should that ever slip my mind, then Kafka is there, axe in hand, to remind me. The point, rather, is that the process leading to falling asleep—as distinct from *being* asleep—is a good model for the ambiguous zone between activity and passivity that also characterizes the experience of reading, of becoming vulnerable to the significance of what I face. To succeed, I must let go of myself and let myself fall.

But—and this, too, is essential—I recognize that falling does not happen of its own accord. It needs to be learned, developed, encouraged. While no hard-and-fast rules bring it about, it is no arbitrary process either. I do not merely stumble about the gallery or the text, hoping somehow to hit the right spot from which to read the work and to be read by it. Rather, my movements are shaped by practice and history, which aid me without predicting success.

A process of cultivation puts me in a position to feel both the need for a book that bites and the bite itself, should it happen. To be struck dumb by a passage in Kafka can, of course, result from inattention or incomprehension or stupidity. But it may also happen after years of study; in that case, the muteness will have a different texture, sharper and more baffling.

Saying that opacity is woven into poetic criticism—to poetic making of any kind—names this way of falling, a way akin to falling in love, falling into prayer, or falling for the beauty of the clouds. Since knowing and not-knowing, know-how and don't-know-how, are tightly entwined here, things can go awry. Pitfalls lurk: it comes with the territory that I might fall for a con artist or a two-timer. I expose myself to the risk of disappointment because, in falling, I yield to what could wound me.

Falling into poetic making involves an activity that allows me to slide into a certain passivity, which in turn puts me in a position—actually, a disposition—for becoming active. Thanks to such active passivity (or is it passive activity?) I become vulnerable to poetic significance (and to love, faith, beauty, injustice).

If reading is a way of rendering oneself vulnerable, then this vulnerability is something neither suffered nor simply willed, but something achieved. This differs from a creaturely vulnerability to violence or hunger or shock, which is why Kafka's allegory of reading falters: being vulnerable to the pain I suffer at the death of someone I love is different from being vulnerable to the power of words—not more or less authentic, nor more or less acute, but different.

THE DIFFICULTY, AND THE ECSTASY, OF REALITY

No matter how high the altitude of reflection, an insight must prove itself close to the ground, down where life happens. So, going back once more to my own ground zero: is it a stretch to say that stuttering and fumbling about Kafka's *Trial* takes part in *making*, in making *poetically*? What if adding not a word were the apt way, or one apt way, of responding to a work like this one? What if the techniques of exegesis, honed through years of study, were finally a ruse I contrive to keep myself from looking Kafka's words straight in the eyes? What if descending into the depths of the text and examining its inner workings to grasp its core, along with the other practices of submersion and of submission we scholars learn and teach, were crafty ways of evading a head-on collision with the conundrum—the slap in the face—that is Kafka's writing?

Interpretation would then be not the key that unlocks the riddle of the text but the armor that deflects its force. We seek its cover because the words before us are more than we can handle. Interpretation as deflection, then.

Deflection is a leitmotif in the work of Stanley Cavell, whose voice echoes in these pages in a way that no citation is equipped to acknowledge. His writings are heavy with sadness, a deep, beautiful, and often long-winded sadness at the way his chosen field of philosophy comes face to face with flagrant moments of human existence only to look away. It troubles him how philosophy attempts "to convert the human condition, the condition of humanity, into an intellectual difficulty," how it recasts the burden of this condition, unbearable as it is sometimes, into the bearable form of a conceptual problem.[25]

To Cora Diamond, also a philosopher, this form of deflection marks what she terms "the difficulty of philosophy." Deflection, she writes, is "what happens when we are moved from the appreciation, or attempt at appreciation, of a difficulty of reality to a philosophical or moral problem apparently in the vicinity."[26] The difficulty of philosophy is that it recoils from the difficulty of reality.

When you read Cavell and Diamond, you can come away with the idea that the difficulty of reality—what in the world is too much for words—clusters around hardship. She devotes most of the essay from which I have quoted to death and killing, of both humans and animals. For his part, Cavell does not tire of the theme of pain, his own pain as well as the pain of others, playing it in endless loops over the course of the five hundred tightly printed pages of his *Claim of Reason*.

If the difficulty of reality derived its force solely or mainly from the misery of reality, then the idea would hold little appeal. That is because flagrant instances of something outstripping the concepts and descriptions that come ready to hand—like my moment facing the passage from *The Trial*—do not exhaust themselves in suffering alone. Often, they come as instances of bliss and beauty, of impossible plenitude, of a world bursting with abundance. And even when this abundance contains cruelty, as it always seems to, I can still be grateful for it, for in dislodging my known ways of seeing and feeling and thinking, it opens the path to new ways of acting.

So, I perk up when Cavell glosses the term "difficulty of reality" as ranging "from instances of being struck dumb by sublime beauty, to speechlessness before horror."[27] Horror *and* beauty, then. The beauty is not prettiness but beauty beyond what I can hold by myself, sublime beauty. Diamond, too, grants that besides death and destruction, "instances of goodness or beauty can throw us. I mean that they give us the sense that *this* should not be, that we cannot fit it into the understanding we have of what the world is like. It is wholly inexplicable that it should be; and yet it is" (60). This should not be and yet it is: there is *more* to the world than I allowed, more violence and more beauty, more wickedness and more goodness.

The difficulty of reality is this ecstasy of reality, the place where it surpasses itself through an upsurge of sense and sensation, and often I cannot tell whether this is a surplus of sense or of senselessness.

Another thing that impresses when reading Cavell and Diamond is the fact that what he calls "the condition of humanity" and she "the difficulty of reality" often appear in their writings as instances in literature. Cavell considers the human condition not in the quotidian nakedness in which he or you or I might encounter it, but as it presents itself in *King Lear* or *Othello* or *The Winter's Tale*. For Diamond, the difficulty of reality comprises "experiences in which we take something in reality to be resistant to our thinking it, or possibly to be painful in its inexplicability, difficult in that way, or perhaps awesome and astonishing in its inexplicability" (45–46)—something *in reality* that is too much for us. Yet this reality is not the reality of the street nor of the home nor the office, but that of the words of poets: Diamond's reflections center on chapters from J. M. Coetzee's novel *Elizabeth Costello* and on a poem by Ted Hughes called "Six Young Men." The difficulty of reality—the term itself, she tells us, is John Updike's—is a difficulty encountered in literature.

Is reaching for literature here its own form of deflection? Raising the question (always rhetorically) is something we like to blame on those tin-eared enough to think that poetic language gives us a paler, thinner, and hence more bearable copy of real reality. (Or else on someone with an ear all too finely tuned to poetry, someone sensitive to its intoxicating power who, frightened by himself, feels a keen need to dismiss—to deflect—the poets' way of opening the path to reality, someone like Plato, say.) Literature *can* deflect from reality; who would deny that escapist literature does exist. But do pale, thin versions of the real thing not always exist? *Real* poetry, we like to say in its defense (maybe with a little more conviction vibrating in our voice than needed), real poetry intensifies language and so intensifies reality itself. The real thing gives us the sense "that *this* should not be, that we cannot fit it into the understanding we have of what the world is like. It is wholly inexplicable that it should be; and yet it is." All true. *Lear* and *The Trial* and "Six Young Men" each puts into words what cannot be put into words; each brings into being what should not be: the flaring up of the opacity of things.

And yet. Even when I admit—admit not to prove my theoretical chops but because I have felt it down into my bones—when I admit that Shakespeare's or Kafka's or Coetzee's language can cause me to run out of my own language, I need not also believe that those moments stand at the apex of the difficulty of reality—that nothing else will do if I am to face this difficulty without flinching. The blinding of Gloucester or the shriek of the man with the washerwoman can lead me to think that this is more than I can take, that "*this* should not be." But then there are incomprehensibilities that puncture me in a different way: I fall in love, or learn that a friend's son has taken his life, or become witness to a child being shamed, and in my joy or rage or grief I think: *this* thing, wholly incomprehensible, should not be; and yet it is. I am rendered speechless by such events that resist fitting into the world, as I am by Gloucester's blinding or by the open-mouthed man, yet the bewilderments are not the same. That some assail me with a savagery that gives the pleasures of contemplation and ambivalence no quarter can make the others feel like a respite, even a consolation.

Have I diminished poetic language by noting a difference between incomprehensibilities, by saying that some instances of not knowing how—how to feel, how to speak, how to go on—whiplash me more than others? Have I turned Kafka into a protective shield when I find myself preferring to talk about his words rather than about my wounds? Probably; probably I am using his words. But it is not easy to say if I am also *mis*using them or *ab*using them. For that, I would have to know what the proper uses of literature are, and I don't.

IS POETRY A DEFLECTION FROM LIFE?

There is another question to be asked: When literature, often standing in for all the arts, is taken to be the stage on which "the condition of humanity" and "the difficulty of reality" find their most flagrant expression, has it not been raised to heights from which it is destined to fall? Is it not saddled then with expectations that it is bound to disappoint? Poetic language, like poetic action in general, can do much, more perhaps than we dare imagine, but it cannot do all. It is true that professional readers have a habit of muffling the detonating force of poetry's incomprehensibility by translating it down into manageable problems; that is one form of malpractice. The other lies in aggrandizing what is already potent enough, which only makes you wonder about its potency.

Suppose that Kafka serves me as a deflection; I cannot be certain, but just suppose. (What Shakespeare, Coetzee, and the others do for Cavell and Diamond I am not fit to judge.) The thought leaves me discontented because this description, always also a rebuke, does injury to my experience of the passage that had me in trouble before my students, also of some others in the novel. Even if they do deflect me from an unbearable, unnamable something, Kafka's words do something else too: they take me out of myself and offer me words for an experience I do not know, and had not known I *could* know.

This experience toward which Kafka's words lead me is not—not mainly—an experience of something I could grasp by feeling my way into it with empathy or imagination, say the experience of pressing a washerwoman against my body while shrieking, or of being a washerwoman pressed against a shrieking man staring at the ceiling, or of some other compelling combination of man, washerwoman, shrieking, and staring, or of an allegorical version of these. No, the experience of taking in these lines is itself nameless, itself difficult to bear. It registers—I am repeating myself—an opacity in experience, the experience of the nonnegotiable strangeness of Kafka's lines. They are too much for words and so leave me tongue-tied.

This muteness may not be as raw as the stammer that seizes me when the news of the young man's suicide unhinges me; true. But that does not make the one into a pale, weak likeness of the other. That is because it is no likeness at all. Just as the scene of the man and the washerwoman is no likeness of a scene in the world (paler, fiercer, sadder, or whatever), the disorientation into which it throws me is no copy of a disorientation I know from life. It is different, and one way it is different is that it is less raw. It is prepared. It is assembled and it is crafted. That is what makes it a poetic work: someone managed to fashion ingredients available to all into a shape that brings out a difficulty of reality that I both somehow know—or it would not touch me—and see for the first time. It surpasses what I can hold and is unbearable that way, but it is also funny and beautiful and weird—so much so that I wish to tell you about it.

IN POETRY, NON-KNOWING IS A PRIMAL CONDITION

Have we gotten anywhere? That is never easy to say when you are after opacity; it's the kind of thing you come upon when not looking for it, like ghosts and missing shadows. I started from a stutter that met a fragment of a passage from *The Trial*, a stutter that felt like a failure (because it was). This stutter was an instance, I said, of not knowing how to speak and what to do in the face of such a thing as the passage from Kafka's novel. But then speechlessness seemed like just the *right* response, or *one* right response, to such an exorbitant work, at least the beginning of a response. Failing to speak revealed itself as one apt way of speaking.

That calls forth something we know already, namely, that the issue of succeeding or failing at making sense of Kafka's work comes up only because of the kind of thing it is: a thing that calls for a response. It calls, and therefore it makes sense to feel called—called to make sense of it. That is what it means to say it is a poetic work, a significant thing. In reading the words, I am called to make sense of them, which means becoming the sort of being who hears their call and, in feeling solicited to make sense, speaks about them to you. But mind you, every step of this process, every layer and dimension, is awash with opacity, for I do not know how to manage becoming such a being as that, nor what to say (how to make sense), or whether to speak or to stutter or to remain silent, nor who this "you" is that I address.

And what about the "I" that addresses "you," that is addressing you and has been throughout these pages? Do I know it? That is a question philosophers like to raise ("know thyself!," they press us), but it is of little importance here. What is important is not whether I *know* this "I" but that I *need* it: no poetic criticism—no poetic making—can do without it. If something is too painful or too strange for words, then it is so not in general, but to this being that I am, *here, now*. Only I can feel the power of the encounter: only I can be called by something of significance; only I can feel pressed to tell you about it; and only I can face the dumbfounding insufficiency of not knowing how. No one (no friend nor like-minded community) and no thing (no apparatus, for example) can have the encounter in my place.

But here is the thing: poetic criticism needs the "I," but not the "I" you and I call on every day. The "I" of poetic criticism is not drenched in self-certitude. It does not have total access to the truth of its experience, ready to offer unimpeachable testimony as to "what I really feel" about every topic I face. It does not signal its authenticity by submerging itself in confession and self-revelation; baring the soul is not the path that opens me to intimacy or urgency. On the contrary: I can be flabbergasted by what I encounter only when I hold at bay my everyday self, that fellow whose habits and moods I know far too well. "Revolutionary joy is what comes out of great books," Gilles Deleuze has written, "not the anguishes of our petty narcissism or the terrors of our guilt."[28]

Nor do the signposts of biography confine this "I" of poetic criticism. It is not pinned down by the particulars of my social existence, no matter how often I reassure myself of their solidity by filling them in on forms: name, age, gender, address, profession, race, ethnicity, citizenship, marital status, income. My "social identity," the title under which these instruments of conformity operate, grants me no privileged access to what happens in a poetic encounter: I have no upper hand reading Kafka for being a Jew (or from Prague or a lawyer) nor reading Baldwin for being Black (or gay or Protestant), for the simple reason that—to repeat—the encounter with the work exceeds me and my place in the social world. Which does not mean that my place in this world is of *no* consequence, only that the shape and intensity of my poetic encounter cannot be derived from nor reduced to what at any given time is taken to be my social identity. (Starting with "As a . . ." is a nonstarter.)

Because it is not a record of a solidly shaped experience that merely awaits being "written up," because it is, rather, the arena for developing something that might—*might*—become an experience, criticism worth its name turns me—"my I"—inside out and upside down. Do I know what to say when I set out to speak or write about a novel or a film? I write to find out, also about myself: Why does this phrase, this image keep coming back to me? What seduces me? What am I afraid of? My past, my CV, my place in systems of belonging—none of these serve as reliable guardrails to keep me from veering off the straight and narrow. When it is intimacy with a work I seek, then I could do worse than be guided by the koan "Not knowing is most intimate."

Being stripped of those assets of my personhood that I hold dear—emotional, biographical, and social assets—is an act of violence to which I open myself when I render the frozen sea within me vulnerable to the axe of the poetic. This dispossession can leave me reeling, but it can also unshackle me: of my appetites and aversions, my social standing, my ambitions, my regrets, my solidarity with groups and causes, my knowledge even. Look at what preoccupies Roland Barthes as he reflects on the way he views photographs:

> I saw clearly that I was concerned here with the impulses of an over-ready subjectivity, inadequate as soon as articulated: *I like/I don't like*: we all have our secret chart of tastes, distastes, indifferences, don't we? But just so: I have always wanted to remonstrate with my moods; not to justify them; still less to fill the scene of the text with my individuality; but on the contrary, to offer, to extend this individuality to a science of the subject, a science whose name is of little importance to me, provided it attains . . . to a generality which neither reduces nor crushes me.[29]

Yes, we have our likes and dislikes, but sometimes it seems that that is all we have, that the entirety of our personhood consists in registering, over and over, "like" or "don't like": like this picture, love that movie, not a fan of this policy, detest that celebrity. It is true that a poetic encounter can be "a blow on the skull," as Kafka wrote in the letter to his friend, but being cracked open this way can also unburden me of my closeness to my attitudes and desires, if only for moments.

We come upon versions of this idea in other writers, and though they speak of poets or artists, we have learned to enlarge the insight to include the poetic critic. The poet, T. S. Eliot writes, suffers "a continual surrender of himself . . . , a continual self-sacrifice, a continual extinction of personality," but this loss promises immense gain. Poetic making, he continues, "is not a turning loose of emotion, but an escape from emotion; it is not the expression of personality, but an escape from personality." And, being Eliot, he adds, "But, of course, only those who have personality and emotions know what it means to want to escape from these things."[30] Paul Celan renders the thought in the pithiest form I know: "Art makes for distance from the I." In German, you can say that in three words: "Kunst schafft Ich-Ferne."[31] "Art creates I-distance," a distance that permits the I release from the liabilities of being too close to itself. One last quote, this from Deleuze: "Literature begins only when a third person is born in us that strips us of the power to say 'I'"; if a writer is to write in a new language, Deleuze says, "the self must be destroyed."[32]

How often have Eliot, Celan, and Deleuze, personages as different in temperament and style as one could wish, gathered in the same paragraph to reach for the same thought? It is a thought with which we have been trying to become friends since we encountered it in Gaston Bachelard's phrase: "in poetry, non-knowing is a primal condition." The non-knowing of poetry describes, *also* describes, the way I forget myself.

Where has this train of thought taken us? To a place quite unlike the workshop of scholarship and science. Where these strive for mastery, poetic criticism seeks intimacy. Where these interrogate the work as to its meaning, poetic criticism looks for ways to take part in the work and continue it. Where these produce and transmit knowledge about their object of study, poetic criticism seeks a surrender of knowledge, not to launch from a place of ignorance nor to land there, but so that the I of criticism has a chance of orienting itself toward the truth.

THE SOCIAL FORCE OF THE IMPERSONAL

Eliot's "continual extinction of personality," Celan's "I-distance," the destruction of the self that Deleuze enjoins—these images reach for the way a hard-shelled I is liquidated—liquified—in poetic experience to yield not a new subject (one equipped with more liberality, more cosmopolitanism, more empathy, more *Bildung*) but a vulnerable pliancy that might be shaped into new arrangements of feelings, memories, desires, and thoughts. (*Might*, not *will*.) At heart, it is a practice of askesis in which I am exposed to an encounter, an encounter too harrowing or too euphoric or too meaningful for my resources, leading, perhaps, to new modes of experience that stretch and multiply my ways of being in the world. Again, a form of opacity issues into poetic making.

There is another, equally basic dimension to this process, a dimension involving you. It is the dimension that orients criticism—orients any sort of poetic making—toward what lies beyond me, toward you and society. If something speaks to me forcefully enough that I feel urged to tell you, then how might what I say (or do or make) speak to you in the same way, prompting you to put down this book, for example, to tell someone? How might it set in motion your own ways of doing and making?

What I say has a chance of moving you (and moving you may well take the form of *stopping* you) if it has force, and it gains force if I find some Richterian strategy of leaping over my own shadow to create distance from my self, to leave behind this self long enough to surpass it. This strategy has a shot at succeeding not because you find my asceticism impressive, but because the "continual extinction of personality" lays bare not a nothingness but the *im*personality in my person, what in all my private wants and wishes is unprivate—is *public*—in me.

If I knew myself fully, then I would remain alien to you. But in truth, I am a stranger to myself, and an account of my encounter with a significant thing manages to speak to you if it testifies to the ways that I find my own resources outstripped. The place where I am a stranger to myself—this impersonality in my person—coincides with the place where my speech and my making cease to be mine alone and open to a public dimension. The opacity to myself is a blockage, yes, but it is also a catapult: it launches me into a world replete with other human beings, with language, desire, technology, power, history, and other dimensions of human existence.

It is, I think, just this impersonality in the person that Roland Barthes seeks in his writings. When he tells us "I have always wanted to remonstrate with my moods" or when he works to check "the impulses of an overready subjectivity," it is to achieve "a generality which neither reduces nor crushes me." This is a generality that does not transform the "I" into a nameless "one" or an amalgamated "we." Like impersonality, it is not the average or the normal or the ideal. The term "generality" (*généralité* in the original) may not be the most apt, since to my ear the point of generalizing lies precisely in flattening the wrinkles of the particular. Deleuze seems to see it the same way, which is why he distinguishes generality from impersonality: literature, he writes, "exists only when it discovers beneath apparent persons the power of an impersonal—which is not a generality but a singularity of the highest point."[33] To further confuse things, elsewhere Barthes speaks of "science" instead of a (nonreductive, noncrushing) generality:

> Perhaps it is finally at the heart of this subjectivity, of this very intimacy which I have invoked, perhaps it is at the "pinnacle of my particularity" that I am scientific without knowing it, vaguely oriented toward that *Scienza Nuova* Vico spoke of.[34]

None of these terms—generality, impersonality, science—captures perfectly what it seeks to name. We should therefore not let their differences trip us up, since the total movement of the passages in which they appear takes us toward the same phenomenon, namely, that "it is at the pinnacle of the particular that the general blossoms." (That is Marcel Proust writing to a school friend.[35]) The poetic can flare up only in the singular—here, now, in *this* thing—but when it flares up, it illuminates a region of significance beyond itself. This enlargement is attained not by thinning out the singular, not by reducing or crushing it through generality, but by reinforcing its singularity through intensification: it can then become "a singularity of the highest point," "the pinnacle of the particular." Nothing else is meant by the urgency of poetic speech.

Saying that poetic speech bears the signature of the writer on every sentence, though the word "I" may never be uttered, does not mean that it appears as an absolute individuality, a configuration unlinked from all else. Were that so, it would not signify but just baffle. Signatures manifest their individuality through systems of meaning, through nations and cultures and history: There are French and English and Japanese signatures. There are masculine and feminine signatures, signatures of the young and of the old, bold signatures and meek ones. Some writing (or marks of any kind) seeks to suppress its signature because it wishes to speak in the pallid Voice of Science (or of Law, of Administration, of the State). That, I think, is Barthes's nemesis. Then there is writing with a signature that puts on display its membership in a tribe or guild. Even its insistence on being "unique" reveals little more than its typicality. And then there is the poetic signature: it remonstrates against the impulses of an overready individuality to reach for the power of the impersonal beneath the person, not by exhibiting the "true me" but by surrendering to the recognition that a signature always says more than the signer knows.

The impersonal within the singular—Kant, using different terms but aiming to grasp the same thing, calls it "subjective universality"—is the way that a thing made poetically calls to me. My experience therefore remains opaque to me for the same reason that it opens to you. Any account I wish to give of having been stopped in my tracks by something that holds an excess of significance—call it a "reading"— must unfurl in such a way that the most private layers of experience come to reveal what is most public. This is how I understand what Emerson says about the poet:

> He then learns, that in going down into the secrets of his own mind, he has descended into the secrets of all minds. . . . The poet, in utter

> solitude remembering his spontaneous thoughts and recording them, is found to have recorded that, which men in crowded cities find true for them also. . . . The deeper he dives into his privatest, secretest presentiment, to his wonder he finds, this is the most acceptable, most public, and universally true. The people delight in it; the better part of every man feels, This is my music; this is myself.[36]

That—all that—is the beauty of it.

Not-knowing-how, essential to poetic criticism, is not my private failing, safeguarded in my sovereign separateness, but one you could come to know. Unlike the blank incomprehension I feel when some event, inordinate in its scale, has befallen me, the incomprehension of the shriek of the man pulling close the washerwoman is one I might be able to share with you. After all, the incomprehension happens with and because of you; it happens because I open my mouth to tell you about it. One reason, then, to go to moments of poetic flagrancy when trying to glimpse the ecstatic difficulty of reality is that, while unbearable, they are impersonal, "most public, and universally true," as Emerson asserts; they are sharable, and essentially so. It is what makes them bearably unbearable.

Sharable does not mean shared. Sharable means: it is not mad to wish to tell you about the way the strangeness or the beauty of some lines left me dazed, with an eye not to offloading the feeling of strangeness and of beauty but to holding it together. It is not mad because reading Kafka or looking at a painting by Richter is the sort of experience that has built into it the wish to tell you; call it an invitation or an obligation. The news of the friend's death does not, not right away: it has no rhyme or reason, no structure and no name, which is why it announces itself with a howl. One day it might turn into something that I can share with you, dulled into the language of an obituary or an anecdote. Yet sometimes—those are rare moments—it can become the occasion for something structured and no longer nameless that has the power to overwhelm with its own strangeness and beauty. Then it is a bit of poetry, sharable not because it is a paler and thinner replica of my "real" grief or fear, but because it reaches a way of knowing and feeling that is not mine alone, whose power to surpass me might surpass you too.

Again, sharable does not mean shared, which just means that things can go awry. In turning to tell you, I risk failing to share the experience with you, because I have botched the telling or because you are in no mood to hear. And that failure can leave me lonelier than not telling you of something I never expected to share.

That may have been another reason why I withheld from you the passage from *The Trial*: it may well not do to you what it does to me (or did that day); it may leave you indifferent or cold, puzzled at the fuss I am making. Which is when a distance opens between us. "Art is often praised because it brings men together," Cavell has written. "But it also separates them."[37] And it is able to separate for the same reason it can bring together, namely, that the call I hear in art—and not in art alone: in all poetic works—has society built into it. When it is achieved, it brings us closer, yet when that society remains unachieved, then we are not just where we began; we have drifted apart. Perhaps we were sitting side by side companionably, each minding our own business, but now the loneliness of an unconsummated bond has taken up residence between us.

One form of opacity lies in the mystery of why the washerwoman passage spoke to me as it did, but another form lies in the riddle of why it spoke to me but may not to you: why what gets under my skin may no more than brush you, or vice versa. One thing criticism seeks to do is to close the rift that art sometimes opens between us, to help you feel what I felt, to see what I saw, to knock the wind out of you as it was knocked out of me.

To Be Continued . . .

It is never easy to say what criticism is good for. Does *The Trial*—does any novel or painting, does any poetic work—stand in need of criticism? We critics shudder at the question. It gives voice to our deepest, darkest anxiety. The moment we raise it, we feel like parasites feeding on the vitality of others (why else call our own work "secondary"?), and then, piqued, we make up for the self-inflicted slight with a great show of bombast.

Why so touchy? Return to the question: does a poetic work stand in need of criticism? If you hear it not rhetorically but as a real question, you notice how lopsidedly it has been posed. It implies that what finally matters in criticism is the work that is allegedly at issue (the novel, the painting, etc.). Is that so? If the work matters, then it matters—and can only matter—because it matters to *me*, to *some* me. What is at issue is not the work in its splendid aloofness, but the work as *I* grapple with it, here, this morning, in this heat, with these people.

Whether *The Trial* needs it or not, *I* need its criticism—I need to speak about it to you—to make sense of what I am reading, not of the words on the page (I know what they mean, and when in doubt, I can look them up) but of the nameless blend of pleasure, disorientation, associations, and memories that is somehow mixed up with my reading and that ebbs and flows in me, and not just in my head. I need to tell you if I am to have a chance of gaining familiarity with the thoughts and feelings stirred up in this encounter. I need to make sense of what Kafka is doing to me and what I am to do about it.

A lot hinges on hearing "making sense" as a kind of *making*. When I say that in facing Kafka's words I "make sense" of myself, I do not approach this as an interesting theoretical problem for which I seek interesting solutions. Why did the passage from *The Trial* leave me reeling? Why do I find my eyes sliding off the page when reading Thomas Mann? Why can I not put down the Lampedusa novel even on its sixth reading?

These are questions that make it sound as though I were simply curious about myself, yet what they really ask is: How have I *become* the sort of being who is blown away by *The Trial,* bored by *Doctor Faustus,* and entranced by *The Leopard*? And how is it that I am *still* not done with these books nor they with me, that my entanglement with them continues to change me in ways that slip out of my grasp? "Blown away," "bored," and "entranced" are just shorthand for the jumble of thoughts and feelings that good criticism unravels and names. But naming here is creating: I do not refer to something that has an independent existence, but bring it into being as I speak about it. Which, finally, is *why* I speak about it.

What criticism makes, then, as it makes sense of Kafka (or whatever), is a self capable of savoring or suffering the thoughts and feelings that I fashion while doing criticism. If the work must matter to me to unleash its force, then there must be a "me" to which it matters, a me that registers the unleashed force. This me is not just given but must be brought about. Criticism is mostly preoccupied with objects, but surreptitiously it works to create a version of myself perceptive enough, sensitive enough, knowledgeable enough to be moved by those objects.

Is it a better version of myself? Sometimes; sometimes I discover in what I have written or in talking to friends (about a movie, say) a more insightful, more generous, funnier version of the self I usually live with. And then sometimes I come across someone prone to glibness or working too hard to be right.

Maybe that is the difference between better criticism and worse: whether it generates better or worse versions of myself. Maybe good criticism is what makes room for a shrewder and kinder version of myself, and our usual terms of praise ("original," "brilliant," and so on) refer finally not to insights into an object but to the way criticism has stretched and strengthened the good muscles of the self.

If poetic criticism now and again manages to encourage better—wittier, kinder—versions of myself, then that wit and that kindness, too, can spread, bringing about (maybe) wittier and kinder versions of others. These versions, again, may endure, joining the repertoire of possible selves, or they may fade as the impression left by the work bleaches. Either way, the sum of wit and kindness in the world will have increased, if only by a bit and only for a time. Of course, the opposite also holds: if an act of criticism, because of the moves it makes or the mood that pervades it, evokes a jaundiced eye or a sneering voice, then it will embolden those qualities, and now bitterness or snark get a chance to multiply.

I am getting carried away. Next thing, I'll be devising a scheme for personal and social betterment-through-criticism (to *nourish the soul,* to *educate better citizens*). But I am struck, and also disheartened, by the fact that when I turn to speak about something that has spoken to me, I do not know what kind of self will show up. I don't know which version of myself is encouraged and which suppressed. Sometimes criticism does nourish my soul, yet I cannot know when or how, nor how to hang on to that particular soul. And if I fail to predict what shape my own self will take in an encounter, can I then prescribe it to you? Not if I think that I will thereby have furthered general goodness.

Poetic criticism, like other forms of poetic making, does not lend itself to being a tool for bringing about desired outcomes, not because it is deaf to morality and politics, but because it is not a tool. Nor is it an instrument or a method. To be sure, tools, instruments, methods, and techniques are involved. But when I make poetically, I do not so much use these tools and techniques as I outwit myself into being used by them. And lucky that poetic making cannot be put to political service, because if it could, then it would be irresponsible, criminal even, *not* to ensure that it has been harnessed for the right ends. We would be obliged to subject it to the strictest supervision (cf. Plato et al.).

Nonetheless, I *can* prescribe—I can, at least, propose, recommend, urge—poetic criticism to you and on you if I promise no more than an occasion for making what you did not know you were able or allowed to make. That sounds modest but isn't, for this way of making expands freedom not by adding one more item to the collection of freedoms you already possess, but by enlarging the very conception of freedom. You'd learn to develop the freedom of giving yourself over to something that surpasses you. Surpassing you, it prods you to seek ways of acting that you did not know you had in yourself—a fragile and mysterious, a delicious freedom.

Enough urging. Your turn.

Acknowledgments

Work on this book was aided by a sabbatical leave from Indiana University, Bloomington, and a research fellowship granted by its College Arts & Humanities Institute. Thank you, IU. I am also grateful to the Einstein Foundation for appointing me Einstein Visiting Fellow at Freie Universität Berlin, where I was able to work on this book.

Some passages from my article "Criticism and Style," published in *New Literary History* 44 (2013), reappear here, mostly rewritten. A few sections in Part 2 were first published as "Schlegel's Words, Rightly Used," in *Poetic Critique: Encounters with Art and Literature*, ed. Michel Chaouli et al. (Berlin: de Gruyter, 2021), 19–34.

When I discovered that my friends Jonathan Elmer and Andrew H. Miller were setting out to write a book just when I was, the plan was hatched that every other Friday we would email the others what we had written the previous two weeks, however paltry the prose. At first, I thought of this as a way of keeping pace. Little did I know how utterly Jonathan and Andrew would come to shape this book. The comments with which they annotated my biweekly installments were models of editorial craft: learned, sharp, witty, generous, no-nonsense. But they were also more than that. Somehow, they brought to light better versions of what I had written. It dawned on me that they were ideal examples of poetic criticism, the very thing I was writing about— *trying* to write about. What I was seeking was right there on the page, squeezed into the comments bubbles of Microsoft Word. Now my task was clear: to write a book that lives up to its first readers. For Jonathan and Andrew then.

Notes

To Start

1. *The Diary of Virginia Woolf*, vol. 2, ed. A. O. Bell (New York: Harcourt Brace, 1978), 129. Andrew H. Miller pointed me to this marvelous passage.

2. Stanley Cavell, "Music Discomposed," in *Must We Mean What We Say?* (Cambridge: Cambridge University Press, 1976), 192.

3. Friedrich Schlegel, "On Goethe's *Meister*," trans. Peter Firchow, in *Classic and Romantic German Aesthetics*, ed. J. M. Bernstein (Cambridge: Cambridge University Press, 2003), 281; translation modified.

Part 1

1. Erich Auerbach, *Mimesis: The Representation of Reality in Western Literature*, trans. Willard R. Trask (Princeton, NJ: Princeton University Press, 2003), 9.

2. James Baldwin, "Everybody's Protest Novel," in *Notes of a Native Son* (Boston: Beacon Press, 1958), 13.

3. Roland Barthes, *Empire of Signs*, trans. Richard Howard (New York: Hill and Wang, 1982), 20–22.

4. Kenneth Burke, "Othello: An Essay to Illustrate a Method," *Hudson Review* 4, no. 2 (1951): 178.

5. Michel Foucault, *The Order of Things* (London: Tavistock/Routledge, 1970), 17–18.

6. Pauline Kael, "Tumescence as Style," *New Yorker*, September 24, 1990.

7. Susan Sontag, "Against Interpretation," in *Against Interpretation and Other Essays* (New York: Farrar Straus, 1966), 9.

8. Martin Heidegger, *Einführung in die Philosophie, Gesamtausgabe*, vol. 27 (Frankfurt: Vittorio Klostermann, 1996), 22.

9. Stanley Cavell, "Music Discomposed," in *Must We Mean What We Say?* (Cambridge: Cambridge University Press, 1976), 197–98.

10. Roland Barthes, *The Rustle of Language*, trans. Richard Howard (Oxford: Blackwell, 1986), 282.

11. Barthes, *Rustle of Language*, 284.

12. Kurt Koffka, *The Growth of the Mind: An Introduction to Child Psychology*, trans. Robert Morris Ogden (London: Kegan Paul, 1924), 319; translation modified.

160 NOTES

13. Maurice Merleau-Ponty, *Phenomenology of Perception*, trans. Colin Smith (London: Routledge & Kegan Paul, 1962), 23–24. (In the 2002 reprint, the passage is on page 27.)

14. Paul de Man, *Allegories of Reading* (New Haven, CT: Yale University Press, 1979), 58.

15. On love and attachment, see Rita Felski, *The Limits of Critique* (Chicago: University of Chicago Press, 2015), 17; on paranoid versus reparative reading, see Eve Kosofsky Sedgwick, *Touching Feeling: Affect, Pedagogy, Performativity* (Durham, NC: Duke University Press, 2003), chap. 4.

16. De Man, *Allegories of Reading*, ix.

17. Paul Ricoeur coins the phrase "school of suspicion" in *Freud and Philosophy: An Essay on Interpretation*, trans. Denis Savage (New Haven, CT: Yale University Press, 1970), 32. "Limits of critique" refers to the title of Rita Felski's 2015 book.

18. Theodor Adorno, *Aesthetic Theory*, trans. Robert Hullot-Kentor (London: Continuum, 1997), 338.

19. Heinrich von Kleist, "On the Marionette Theatre," trans. Thomas Neumiller, *TDR: The Drama Review* 16, no. 3 (September 1972): 26.

20. Just one sample passage: "reception . . . is inadequate if it is less reflexive than the object it receives. Not knowing what one sees or hears bestows no privileged direct relation to works but instead makes their perception impossible. Consciousness is not a layer in a hierarchy built over perception; rather, all elements of aesthetic experience are reciprocal," and so on. Adorno, *Aesthetic Theory*, 338.

21. Maurice Merleau-Ponty, "Cézanne's Doubt," in *The Merleau-Ponty Reader*, ed. Ted Toadvine and Leonard Lawlor (Evanston, IL: Northwestern University Press, 2007), 79.

22. Adorno, *Aesthetic Theory*, 334.

23. Susan Sontag, "On Style," in *Against Interpretation and Other Essays*, 22.

24. Hans-Georg Gadamer, "Was ist Wahrheit," in *Gesammelte Werke*, vol. 2 (Tübingen: J. C. B. Mohr, 1993), 55.

25. Hans-Georg Gadamer, *Truth and Method*, 2nd ed., trans. W. Glen-Doepel, rev. Joel Weinsheimer and Donald Marshall (London: Continuum, 2004), 283, 293.

26. James Baldwin, "Stranger in the Village," in *Notes of a Native Son*, 169.

27. James Baldwin, "Many Thousands Gone," in *Notes of a Native Son*, 30.

28. James Baldwin, "Autobiographical Notes," in *Notes of a Native Son*, 6–7.

29. James Baldwin, "Preface to the 1984 Edition," in *Notes of a Native Son*, xiv.

Part 2

1. *The Diary of Virginia Woolf*, vol. 2, ed. A. O. Bell (New York: Harcourt Brace, 1978), 129.

2. Hans-Georg Gadamer, *Truth and Method*, 2nd ed., trans. W. Glen-Doepel, rev. Joel Weinsheimer and Donald Marshall (London: Continuum, 2004), 360.

3. Friedrich Schlegel, "On Goethe's *Meister*," trans. Peter Firchow, in *Classic and Romantic German Aesthetics*, ed. J. M. Bernstein (Cambridge: Cambridge University Press, 2003), 281; translation modified.

4. Hans Ulrich Gumbrecht, *Production of Presence: What Meaning Cannot Convey* (Stanford, CA: Stanford University Press, 2004), xv, 56, 80.

5. Maurice Merleau-Ponty, *Phenomenology of Perception*, trans. Colin Smith (London: Routledge & Kegan Paul, 1962), xviii. (In the 2002 reprint, the passage is on page xx.)

6. Clifford Geertz, *The Interpretation of Cultures* (New York: Basic Books, 1973), 6–7.

7. Ralph Waldo Emerson, "The American Scholar," in *Emerson's Prose and Poetry*, ed. Joel Porte and Saundra Morris (New York: Norton, 2001), 59.

8. Schlegel, "On Goethe's *Meister*," 281; translation modified.

9. Charles Baudelaire, *Oeuvres complètes*, ed. Yves-Gérard Le Dantec, rev. Claude Pichois (Paris: Gallimard, 1961), 877.

10. Friedrich Nietzsche, "On Truth and Lying in a Non-Moral Sense," in *The Birth of Tragedy and Other Writings*, ed. Raymond Geuss and Ronald Spiers, trans. Roland Spiers (Cambridge: Cambridge University Press, 1999), 150.

11. Susan Sontag, "Against Interpretation," in *Against Interpretation and Other Essays* (New York: Farrar Straus, 1966), 7.

12. Schlegel, "On Goethe's *Meister*," 281; translation modified.

13. Walter Benjamin, *Selected Writings*, vol. 2, pt. 1, ed. Michael W. Jennings et al., trans. Rodney Livingstone et al. (Cambridge, MA: Harvard University Press, 1999), 547.

14. Gadamer, *Truth and Method*, 15.

15. D. W. Winnicott, *Playing and Reality* (London: Routledge, 1991), 12, quoted in Jonathan Elmer, "On Not Forcing the Question: Criticism and Playing Along," in *Poetic Critique: Encounters with Art and Literature*, ed. Michel Chaouli et al. (Berlin: de Gruyter, 2021), 66.

16. Elmer, "On Not Forcing the Question."

17. Jean-Paul Sartre, *Anti-Semite and Jew*, trans. George J. Becker (New York: Schocken, 1948), 89.

18. Andrew H. Miller, "Implicative Criticism, or The Display of Thinking," *New Literary History* 44, no. 3 (2013): 345–60.

19. Gadamer, *Truth and Method*, 277.

20. Theodor W. Adorno, *Minima Moralia*, trans. E. F. N. Jephcott (London: Verso, 2005), 36.

21. William Empson, *Argufying: Essays on Literature and Culture*, ed. John Haffenden (Iowa City: University of Iowa Press, 1987), 83.

22. Paul de Man, *Allegories of Reading* (New Haven, CT: Yale University Press, 1979), 58.

23. Jeanne Favret-Saada, *Deadly Words: Witchcraft in den Bocage*, trans. Catherine Cullen (Cambridge: Cambridge University Press, 1980), 4.

24. John Guillory, *Professing Criticism* (Chicago: University of Chicago Press, 2022), 344; Jonathan Kramnick, "Criticism and Truth," *Critical Inquiry* 47 (Winter 2021): 232.

25. Stanley Cavell, "Knowing and Acknowledging," in *Must We Mean What We Say?* (Cambridge: Cambridge University Press, 1976), 257.

26. Friedrich Schlegel, *Lyceum* Fragment 117, in *Philosophical Fragments*, trans.

Peter Firchow (Minneapolis: University of Minnesota Press, 1991), 14–15; translation modified.

27. One response to the fragment can be found in my essay "'We Hear That We May Speak': Overtures for Doing Criticism," *Arcadia: International Journal of Literary Culture*, forthcoming. Some passages from that essay reappear here.

28. Emerson, "American Scholar," 60.

29. Elena Ferrante, *My Brilliant Friend*, trans. Ann Goldstein (New York: Europa Editions, 2012), 130.

30. Friedrich Nietzsche, *The Gay Science*, ed. Bernard Williams, trans. Josefine Nauckhoff (Cambridge: Cambridge University Press, 2001), 90.

31. John Williams, *Stoner* (New York: New York Review Books, 2003), 98.

32. Gaston Bachelard, *The Poetics of Space*, trans. Maria Jolas (New York: Penguin, 2014), 11.

33. J. L. Austin, for example, writes apropos of poetry: "There are parasitic uses of language, which are 'not serious,' not the 'full normal use.'" *How to Do Things with Words* (Oxford: Oxford University Press, 1962), 104.

34. Bachelard, *Poetics of Space*, 11.

35. Immanuel Kant, *Critique of the Power of Judgment*, trans. Paul Guyer and Eric Matthews (Cambridge: Cambridge University Press, 2000), 284–85 (using the pagination of the *Akademie* edition).

36. Gilles Deleuze, "Literature and Life," in *Essays Critical and Clinical*, trans. Daniel W. Smith and Michael A. Greco (London: Verso, 1998), 4.

37. Kant, *Critique of the Power of Judgment*, 211.

38. Emerson, "American Scholar," 64.

39. Friedrich Schlegel, *Die Entwicklung der Philosophie in zwölf Büchern* (1804–1805), in *Kritische Friedrich Schlegel Ausgabe*, vol. 12, ed. Jean-Jacques Anstett (Paderborn: Schöningh, 1964), 371.

40. Even Theodor Adorno, as constant an advocate of the aesthetic sphere as one is likely to find among philosophers, considers their "semblance character" to be an essential feature of works of art. Adorno, *Aesthetic Theory*, trans. Robert Hullot-Kentor (London: Continuum, 1997), 103.

41. Immanuel Kant, *Groundwork of the Metaphysics of Morals*, in *Practical Philosophy*, trans. and ed. Mary J. Gregor (Cambridge: Cambridge University Press, 1996), 447 (using the pagination of the *Akademie* edition).

42. Emerson, "American Scholar," 59.

Part 3

1. To see a reproduction, google "Andreas Gursky 99 Cent" or go to www.andreasgursky.com/en/works/1999/99-cent.

2. Immanuel Kant, *Critique of Pure Reason*, my translation of *Gängelwagen der Urteilskraft* (p. 134 in 1st ed., 174 in 2nd).

3. Franz Kafka, *The Trial*, trans. Breon Mitchell (New York: Schocken, 1998), 51.

4. G. W. F. Hegel, *Aesthetics: Lectures on Fine Art*, trans. T. M. Knox (Oxford: Oxford University Press), 1:153.

5. Ludwig Wittgenstein, *Bemerkungen über die Philosophie der Psychologie/Remarks on the Philosophy of Psychology*, bilingual ed., trans. G. E. M. Anscombe, ed. G. E. M. Anscombe and G. H. von Wright (Oxford: Basil Blackwell, 1980), 1:156. I translate *Mitteilung* as "communication" rather than "information."

6. T. S. Eliot, "Tradition and the Individual Talent," in *Selected Essays* (London: Faber and Faber, 1934), 15.

7. Gaston Bachelard, *The Poetics of Space*, trans. Maria Jolas (New York: Penguin, 2014), 17.

8. Viktoria von Flemming, *Gerhard Richter: Meine Bilder sind klüger als ich* (1992), a TV documentary made for Norddeutscher Rundfunk.

9. George Saunders, "What Writers Really Do When They Write," *Guardian*, March 4, 2017.

10. John Williams, *Stoner* (New York: New York Review Books, 2003), 98.

11. Immanuel Kant, *Critique of the Power of Judgment*, trans. Paul Guyer and Eric Matthews (Cambridge: Cambridge University Press, 2000), 308 (using the pagination of the *Akademie* edition). I unpack this idea in chapter 5 of my book *Thinking with Kant's Critique of Judgment* (Cambridge, MA: Harvard University Press, 2017).

12. Gilles Deleuze, *Essays Critical and Clinical*, trans. Daniel W. Smith and Michael A. Greco (London: Verso, 1998), 109–10.

13. Immanuel Kant, *Anthropology from a Pragmatic Point of View*, trans. Robert Louden, in *Anthropology, History, and Education*, ed. Günter Zöller and Robert Louden (Cambridge: Cambridge University Press, 2007), 7:220 (using the pagination of the *Akademie* edition); translation modified.

14. Eve Kosofsky Sedgwick, "Paranoid Reading and Reparative Reading," in *Touching Feeling: Affect, Pedagogy, Performativity* (Durham, NC: Duke University Press, 2003).

15. Ralph Waldo Emerson, "The American Scholar," in *Emerson's Prose and Poetry*, ed. Joel Porte and Saundra Morris (New York: Norton, 2001), 60; Walter Benjamin, fragment written in 1931, trans. Rodney Livingstone, in *Selected Writings*, vol. 2, pt. 2, ed. Howard Eiland, Michael Jennings, and Gary Smith (Cambridge, MA: Harvard University Press, 1999), 547; Stanley Cavell, "Music Discomposed," in *Must We Mean What We Say?* (Cambridge: Cambridge University Press, 1976), 193.

16. Novalis, Miscellaneous Observation 125, in *Philosophical Writings*, trans. and ed. Margaret Mahony Stoljar (Albany: State University of New York Press, 1997), 45; translation modified.

17. Novalis, Miscellaneous Observation 68, in *Philosophical Writings*, 34.

18. Friedrich Schlegel, *Athenäum* Fragment 22, in *Philosophical Fragments*, trans. Peter Firchow (Minneapolis: University of Minnesota Press, 1991), 21.

19. Schlegel, *Athenäum* Fragment 24, in *Philosophical Fragments*.

20. Walter Benjamin, *The Concept of Criticism in German Romanticism*, trans. David Lachterman, Howard Eiland, and Ian Balfour, in *Selected Writings*, vol. 1, ed. Marcus Bullock and Michael Jennings (Cambridge, MA: Harvard University Press, 1996), 153.

21. Benjamin, *Concept of Criticism*, 153; translation modified.

22. Shoshana Felman develops this thought in her book *Jacques Lacan and the*

Adventure of Insight: Psychoanalysis in Contemporary Culture (Cambridge, MA: Harvard University Press, 1987), esp. 22–23.

23. Franz Kafka, *Letters to Friends, Family and Editors*, trans. Richard and Clara Winston (New York: Schocken, 1977), 16; translation modified.

24. Maurice Merleau-Ponty, *Phenomenology of Perception*, trans. Colin Smith (London: Routledge & Kegan Paul, 1962), 163–64. (In the 2002 reprint, the passage is on pages 189–90.)

25. Stanley Cavell, *The Claim of Reason* (Oxford: Oxford University Press, 1979), 493.

26. Cora Diamond, "The Difficulty of Reality and the Difficulty of Philosophy," in Stanley Cavell et al., *Philosophy and Animal Life* (New York: Columbia University Press, 2008), 57.

27. Stanley Cavell, "Companionable Thinking," in Cavell et al., *Philosophy and Animal Life*, 92.

28. Gilles Deleuze, "Nomad Thought," trans, Jacqueline Wallace, *semiotexte* 3, no. 1 (1977): 19.

29. Roland Barthes, *Camera Lucida*, trans. Richard Howard (New York: Hill and Wang, 1981), 18.

30. Eliot, "Tradition and the Individual Talent," 17; 21.

31. Paul Celan, "Der Meridian, Rede anläßlich der Verleihung des Georg-Büchner-Preises," in *Gesammelte Werke*, vol. 3, ed. Beda Allemann et al. (Frankfurt: Suhrkamp, 1983), 193; "The Meridian: Speech on the Occasion of Receiving the Georg-Büchner Prize, Darmstadt, 22 October 1960," in *Collected Prose*, trans. Rosemarie Waldrop (Manchester: Carcanet Press, 1986), 44.

32. Deleuze, *Essays Critical and Clinical*, 3, 113.

33. Deleuze, *Essays Critical and Clinical*, 3.

34. Roland Barthes, *The Rustle of Language*, trans. Richard Howard (Oxford: Blackwell, 1986), 290.

35. July 19, 1919, www.library.illinois.edu/rbx/letter-from-marcel-proust-to-daniel-halevy-19-july-1919.

36. Emerson, "American Scholar," 64.

37. Cavell, "Music Discomposed," 193.

Index